MW00627801

The Complete Guide to Shih Tzu Dogs

Molly Weinfurter

LP Media Inc. Publishing

Text copyright © 2019 by LP Media Inc.

www.lpmedia.org

Publication Data

Molly Weinfurter

The Complete Guide to Shih Tzu Dogs ---- First edition.

Summary: "Successfully raising a Shih Tzu dog from puppy to old age" --- Provided by publisher.

ISBN: 978-179-659910-7

[1. Shih Tzu --- Non-Fiction] I. Title.

Design by Sorin Rădulescu

First paperback edition, 2019

TABLE OF CONTENTS

CHAPTER 1
What Is a Shih Tzu?

If you've ever seen the small show dogs with long hair that drags on the floor like a mop, they are most likely a Shih Tzu. In other words, they are known to be fancy, well-groomed dogs that are typically seen with a bow in their hair. This is how many people picture a Shih Tzu, but the truth is that this breed is so much more than that. They don't need to have long, flowing hair or fancy ribbons in their ears all the time because they are not just a show dog, but also a common everyday pet. For those who are unfamiliar with this breed, it may be difficult to distinguish them from other small, fluffy dogs, but once you get to know a Shih Tzu, its unique characteristics will make it stand out from all other breeds. They are an excellent companion dog for a wide range of people due to their sweet nature and lovable personality.

Photo Courtesy of Erin Abay

Physical Characteristics

"An interesting fact is that a Shih Tzu may completely change colors. If you buy a Shih Tzu based on color, you may be disappointed in a few months to find the dog looks completely different. For example, it is common that a solid dark chocolate Shih Tzu puppy, may become a milky gray or cream colored within the year."

Twila Severance
Divine Design Shih Tzu

Shih Tzu have a unique appearance because they have a large variety of different traits. Not all Shih Tzu look exactly alike. Many people tend to confuse them with other small breeds such as the Lhasa Apso or the Havanese, but there several ways to tell a Shih Tzu apart from similar dogs. Even though not all Shih Tzu look alike, the breed shares multiple common traits. For example, they can typically be distinguished by their flat, round faces. While most dog breeds have a long snout, the Shih Tzu is one of the few breeds with a nose that almost appears to be squished up against their face. Examples of other breeds that have this flatter face are Pugs and Pekingese.

As for their coloring, Shih Tzu don't have one main color. They come in a wide variety of colors and coat patterns. Common colors for Shih Tzu are white, brown, black, gray, and brindle. Oftentimes, they will be a mixture of more than one color, such as black and white or brown and white. If they are two different colors, then they typically will have unique patterns such as large and small spots throughout their coat.

Since Shih Tzu shed very little, their coat is considered hair instead of fur. This means that their hair grows and needs to be cut just as a human's hair would. Their hair can be whatever length the owner prefers, but many people like to keep their Shih Tzu dogs hair short. Shorter hair allows the Shih Tzu to move around more freely and requires less brushing and maintaining than longer hair. Another common style is to keep the hair longer only on the top of the Shih Tzu's head, so that the hair can be clipped with a bow or ribbon. As a pet, their hair can still be kept long like a show dog, but the longer their hair is, the more difficult it is to maintain. A Shih Tzu typically needs to be groomed fairly often to maintain their coat, no matter the length. Luckily, this means that their hair is almost always soft.

One of the most distinguishing features on a Shih Tzu is their eyes. They tend to have large eyes that stick out of their head a little bit. Sometimes their eyes appear to almost be going in two different directions. It can make them look a bit crazy or silly, but in an adorable way, of course. An under-bite is another common trait among Shih Tzu. This means that their bottom teeth stick so far forward that they are almost always visible. Not all Shih Tzu have an underbite and they are not the only breed that can have it, but it is a well-known trait for them. Breeders will often try to avoid getting puppies with an underbite because it could cause health issues in the future and it looks a little odd. But for the most part, it just adds some personality to your pup and makes them look like they're constantly smiling.

Shih Tzu are categorized as small dogs because they typically weigh anywhere from nine to sixteen pounds and are between eight and eleven inches high. Their legs are usually fairly short and their bodies can look a bit round even if they are a healthy weight. This body type causes them to grow tired very easily, which is why they are commonly known as a lazier breed. Even so, make sure they get plenty of exercise because it is easy for this calm breed to gain some extra weight.

Despite being a small breed, Shih Tzu are typically a fairly solid dog. When you reach to pick one up, you may be surprised by how hefty they are. Just because they feel a little bit on the heavier side does not necessarily mean they are overweight though. It is usually just the way the breed is built.

Photo Courtesy of
Brenda Soto

Behavioral Characteristics

While Shih Tzu may resemble other small breeds, their typical personalities can vary greatly from those similar breeds. Similar to most kinds of dogs, a Shih Tzu's personality varies from dog to dog. While there are some common traits among this breed, it is good to remember that not every Shih Tzu will act exactly the same. One example of a common Shih Tzu trait is their loyalty. Once they find a home, they quickly grow close to their family. This typically means that they will want to spend as much time with you as possible, and they get excited every time they see you. When left alone, they will often try to find your dirty laundry to sleep in so that they can still smell you. They'll do anything they can to be by your side as much as possible.

QUOTE
"Little Lion"

The little Shih Tzu is a perfect lapdog for a family with children, singles, or senior citizens. This little dog, 9-10 inches and 9-16 lbs., will honor his owner with loyalty and companionship for many years. The life span of a Shih Tzu is between 10-18 years and can depend on the quality of care he is given during his life. Although a Shih Tzu's coat may be high maintenance, the owner will be rewarded with a beautiful, silky "little lion" once revered by Chinese royalty.

This strong loyalty also means that Shih Tzu are very protective of the people they are close to. They easily get jealous or worried if they see you around unfamiliar dogs or people. They may growl or snap when they are concerned about others causing harm to you. It is important to train them to fix these habits because even though your Shih Tzu is just looking out for you, other people may think your dog is mean or scary. Despite their small size, Shih Tzu can act tough when they need to be.

Another characteristic that many Shih Tzu share is stubbornness. They do not like to be bossed around or told what to do, so sometimes training them can be a bit difficult. They are very set in their ways, so it is important to always be patient with them when trying to get them to listen to you. Make sure you're the one training them and not vice versa. They are sneaky and will try to get you to do what they want. For example, even if they can easily jump up on a bed or couch, they may learn that if they sit and whine, you will pick them up yourself. It's a lazy habit, but many Shih Tzu catch on to things like this, so be careful that your new dog doesn't try to boss you around.

Photo Courtesy of
Judi Gullickson

Shih Tzu are not one of the dog breeds that are known to have high intelligence. Training can be confusing for them and sometimes they don't even notice something right in front of their face, but they are wise in other ways. They can tell when their owner is upset and they know exactly how to comfort them. They may not be able to do an elaborate talent show act, but at least they know how to be a great companion.

While some of these common characteristics may come across as a bit negative, that is not the case at all. These traits are unique to this breed and give them an interesting and entertaining personality. There is almost never a boring day with a Shih Tzu by your side. Even if they sound like they can be a lot to handle, it is important to remember that they are a very loving and friendly breed. They love to meet new people and they get excited every time someone is willing to pet them. Because of their sweet and loyal nature, Shih Tzu are also great therapy and emotional support pets. They are guaranteed to cheer up anyone who stops to pet them, especially their owners and any other people whom they have grown to trust.

While you will need a lot of patience with your dog and the training process can be slow, Shih Tzu are a playful and friendly breed that will bring joy to your life if this is the breed you decide to get.

The History of the Shih Tzu

There is record of Shih Tzu going back for at least one thousand years. They originated in China, primarily in Tibet, where they were referred to as "the Lion Dog." This is because their hair was kept long to resemble a lion's mane. These dogs were common in the Buddhist religion, due to the fact that lions were a significant part of their culture. Since there were no actual lions in China, they decided to breed these small dogs to look like them.

Shih Tzu were bred to be companion dogs, specifically to warm the feet of royalty. They were typically found lounging around the palace of the Emperor of China to keep royalty company. One of their main roles in the palace was to keep watch for unwanted visitors and to bark if they saw any unfamiliar people or animals.

FUN FACT

The Shih Tzu has a long and regal history. The beloved Shih Tzu was bred for the laps of Chinese royalty beginning over 2000 years ago. The little "lion dog" is commonly thought to have been developed by Tibetan Monks for the emperors of China. These small imperial dogs lived quietly inside palace walls until the 1930s when they were first introduced in Europe. Shih Tzu breed clubs began forming in Peking and across Europe. First classified as "Apsos," the AKC recognized the Shih Tzu breed, and a Shih Tzu Kennel Club of England was formed in 1935. The AKC ranks this little bundle of love and joy in the top 20 dog breeds.

Over time, the Shih Tzu breed has not changed too drastically. Now, they are a common household pet instead of only companions for royalty, but many of their characteristics have remained constant. The breed is still used as a companion dog, and they still prefer to comfort their owners as much as possible. Shih Tzu are also still protective of their owners and like to bark when they see unwanted visitors near their home, which could be related to the way the breed protected emperors all those years ago.

Is a Shih Tzu the Right Fit for You?

Shih Tzu are a great pet to have, but they may not be the right choice for everyone. So, how do you know if a Shih Tzu is the right breed for you?

First off, make sure a small dog is ideally what you're looking for. Even if you love all dogs, most people have a strong preference for either large or small breeds. A small breed such as a Shih Tzu may be a great fit for you if you live in a smaller house or apartment and don't have enough space for a larger dog to run around. If you travel a lot and are hoping to bring your dog with you, a small dog is easier to travel with. Shih Tzu are especially travel-friendly since they generally are a laid-back breed. Another reason people prefer smaller dogs is simply because they are easier to pick up and cuddle. They don't take much strength to hold in your arms and if they won't cooperate at any point, you can just pick them up and take them with you.

Another reason a Shih Tzu might be the right fit for you is if you're looking for a hypoallergenic dog. People who are allergic to dogs are mainly allergic to the fur and drool that come off of the dog, but luckily Shih Tzu don't shed or drool any more than the average person does. So, if you are close to anyone who has allergies, you probably do not have to worry about your new Shih Tzu being a problem when they come to visit. Also, it is easier to keep your house and your clothes clean when you don't have to worry about dog fur getting everywhere.

Some people think getting a small, laid-back breed such as a Shih Tzu means that they don't need to give them as much attention, but that is not accurate at all. Shih Tzu love attention and if you give your dog only a minimal amount of it, then they will become bored or lonely. It is im-

portant to understand that choosing to adopt a Shih Tzu is a big decision and they need to be treated with just as much love and attention as any other dog.

Not only are Shih Tzu a small, hypoallergenic breed, but there are other factors that can help show whether or not they are the ideal breed for you. More specifically, a Shih Tzu is the right dog for you if you are looking for a companion dog that will bond quickly with you. You need to be open to a dog that can be very playful and energetic sometimes while other times can be lazy and sleepy. You also need to be willing to be patient with your Shih Tzu, but overall the benefits of having a Shih Tzu as a pet greatly outweigh the negatives.

CHAPTER 2
Choosing a Shih Tzu

A lot of factors go into choosing the ideal Shih Tzu. It is important to decide which method is best for you, whether it is buying a newborn puppy or adopting from either a local shelter or dog rescue. No matter which path you decide to take, be patient with your decision. Remember, this dog is not just like any other purchase, because they will soon become a new member of your family.

Buying vs. Adopting

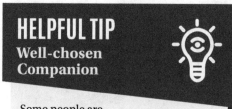

HELPFUL TIP
Well-chosen Companion

Some people are tempted to choose a quiet puppy that sits apart from the others. Maybe the puppy needs love and attention. But be wary when choosing your new friend. Use your head and heart while looking for your new companion. A puppy should be outgoing, playful, and friendly. Look for an active puppy, one that is ready to have fun, and who is energetic. Starting off on the right foot with your new family member, and making sure you are a good fit, is a good investment of your time.

When it comes to choosing a new dog, there are two main options. The first is to adopt a dog, which means you would need to look at a local animal shelter or dog rescue. The second option is to purchase a puppy from a certified breeder. Some people know right away which way is better for them, but sometimes it can be difficult to decide. If you are uncertain which path to take, make sure to consider all of the pros and cons to each method first.

Many people decide to adopt because there are so many dogs out there that are already looking for a loving home. There are lots of local shelters and rescues around, but of course some areas will have more options than others. You can easily search online to get a look at all of the adoptable dogs near you. It's always a good idea to look at your options before trying to buy a new puppy because sometimes the perfect dog is already out there waiting for a home.

The reason people often steer toward breeders instead of rescues is because when adopting, you usually would not be getting a young puppy. You can only adopt what's currently available. Since Shih Tzu are a

popular breed, they can be harder to find in shelters or rescues unless they are a bit older. Also, if you are someone who for sure wants a pure-bred Shih Tzu, then that is much more difficult to come by when adopting a dog. This is because much of the time, rescues and shelters do not know the exact history of the dog.

However, that being said, adopting an adult dog can be better because this usually means that the dog is already housetrained and may even know some basic commands. When raising a new puppy, people often forget how much work will go into caring for that newborn. They will not be trained and it will take a lot of time and patience to properly train them. A full-grown dog will likely take less time to train and adjust since they have probably gone through some type of learning in the past. When visiting rescue dogs, the foster home or shelter can easily tell you how much the dog already knows and how well-behaved they are. Training a puppy can be stressful, but adopting a full-grown dog can take some of that extra work away.

The main reason people often prefer to buy a puppy from a breeder is because from a breeder, you know exactly what you're going to get

Photo Courtesy of Monica Cox

and where your pup is coming from. The breeder will be able to tell you what types of traits the puppies should inherit and will guarantee that your new puppy will be given to you in good health.

Many people also prefer puppies not only because they're adorable, but because you get to raise your new dog throughout that dog's entire life. You get to be with them through every milestone, just like you would be with a child. It can be exciting to see your dog grow as you do. If you're willing to put in the extra time and effort to raise a puppy, then a breeder might be the better choice for you.

Another thing to consider about the two options is that the pricing is drastically different. Breeding the perfect puppy comes at cost. When buying from a breeder, the average price is usually between five hundred and fifteen hundred dollars. Every breeder will price their dogs differently, but generally, the more you pay, the better quality you can expect.

Adopting a Shih Tzu is generally much cheaper, at an average of between one hundred and three hundred dollars. This typically will include the dog being fixed ahead of time as well as all of the required vaccinations. Your rescue dog will also usually be microchipped in case they ever get lost. These things sometimes cost extra when buying a puppy, making adoption much cheaper if money is a big factor on your decision. However, either way, there are pros and cons to each method, so before moving forward, take plenty of time to think about it.

Finding a Reputable Breeder

"A good breeder will ask the potential buyer a ton of questions. They want the best home for their pups."

Marion Starr
Starrme Shihtzu

When purchasing a Shih Tzu puppy, make sure to find a trustworthy breeder. There are tons of different options out there, so simply searching on the internet for one may be frustrating. The huge selection of breeders could make it overwhelming and difficult to decide which choice is the best one for you.

A good way to get specific recommendations on a reputable breeder is to discuss it with someone who works closely with dogs, such as a nearby vet or groomer. They will likely be able to point you in the right direction and give you advice on how to tell whether or not a breeder is reliable and reputable. This can at least help you to greatly narrow down your options. You can also ask around for recommendations from family and friends who have bought Shih Tzu puppies before.

The best breeders will be the ones who know the most about the breed. Since Shih Tzu are a popular breed, people may breed them just to earn a lot of money off of it. These are the breeders that you want to avoid. You want to find someone who is passionate about Shih Tzu because they will be the most trustworthy for you. Therefore, the more informed the breeder is and the more they seem to really care about the breed, the more likely they are to be a good choice.

A good breeder will also want to get to know you better before you adopt a puppy. They will want to make sure their puppies go to a good home and a loving family. If a breeder has very little contact with you outside of purchasing the puppy, they may not be the best option. Don't be afraid to ask as many questions about the process as you want. A trustworthy breeder will want to make sure you are as comfortable as possible before taking your new pet home.

Before deciding on a breeder, it is a good idea to visit different breeders that you're interested in. This will give you a chance to discuss any questions or concerns with the breeders as well as meet the potential parents of your future dog. You want to make sure the parents are in good health and in acceptable living conditions in order to ensure that your puppy will be healthy as well. You also want to make sure that the parents are well trained. If they jump up on you and bark a lot when you come to visit them, then this may be a warning sign. If a breeder is not able to properly train their own dogs, then the chances of them taking good care of your puppy are not as good.

A good breeder will be able to tell you about the traits that will likely be passed down from the parents to your puppy as well as if there are any health concerns you should know about ahead of time. An acceptable breeder will never hold any of this information back and will be more than happy to answer all your questions. If the breeder that you're working with seems unreliable, then don't be afraid to find a different one. The last thing you want is to buy a puppy and then realize it is not what you expected to get.

Most breeders will not allow you to visit the puppies until they are around four weeks of age. If this is the case, don't think that the breeder is being rude and preventing you from meeting your future dog. They only do this for the safety of their puppies. Dogs need time to adjust to the world around them before going home with a new family. However, some breeders will still send you plenty of pictures and will even be willing to video chat with you so you can be kept up to date on how the puppies are doing. If a breeder does not update you on the litter you are interested in, then they may not be a trustworthy source to adopt a puppy from.

Once you've found a breeder, they should provide you with proof that your new puppy is in good health. Most breeders are more than happy to give you proof that your Shih Tzu is a purebred and from a line of healthy and well-bred dogs. However, it is also a good idea to take your puppy to a vet right after you get it, just to verify that everything the breeder said about its health is correct. This way, you know for sure that you got the puppy you were looking for.

Photo Courtesy of
Dr. Troy Clifford Dargin

Choosing the Perfect Puppy

When you see a litter of puppies, they all may seem similar at first, but each will have its own quirks and personality traits. If you only see photos of the puppies ahead of time, you will likely tend to pick the puppy with the coolest coloring, but don't be afraid to change your mind once you meet them. A different puppy might bond with you better, so keeping an open mind will help you to make a better decision in the end. Also, as your puppy grows up, their coloring can slightly change in the first year. Therefore, if you select your pup solely based on their hair pattern, then you may become disappointed as they become a full-grown dog and no longer look the same.

There are certain things you can look for in a litter to help you decide which puppy is the best fit for you. The main areas to focus on when meeting puppies are their activity level, temperament, and health. Not all puppies will be exactly the same in all of these areas.

Shih Tzu do not have a high activity level to begin with, but when looking at puppies, it can be tempting to be drawn toward the one with the most energy. Many people prefer the most playful puppy, but that's not the best option for everyone, so it is important for you to decide which you would prefer. You should be able to tell which puppies have the most energy based on how they interact with each other. Some may run around and play the whole time while others may keep to themselves. There is no right or wrong to which one you choose; it's all based on which one you think will be better for you.

Even though Shih Tzu often share similar personality traits, their temperaments can still vary between each puppy. Some may come right over to you with their tails wagging while others may be a bit more hesitant at first. Try to spend time with each individual puppy to see which one you bond the most with. You may be able to tell right away which one is your ideal dog. Sometimes even the shyest puppies open up to the right people.

Before selecting a puppy to bring home, you should be able to tell whether or not they are in good health. Your new puppy's hair should appear shiny when you see them. If the coat looks dull and doesn't feel very soft when you touch it, this could be a concern. You also will want to make sure that the puppy is a good weight and not skinny or too heavy. Also, check the eyes and ears to make sure they look clean. You want to be certain your pup is as healthy as possible. If you have any concerns about the puppies, don't be afraid to discuss them with the breeder before purchasing one.

Adopting from a Shelter

Photo Courtesy of Renee' Willard

One of the most common ways to adopt a dog is from a local shelter. There are likely multiple different shelters or humane societies in your area, so even if you are hesitant about adopting from a shelter, it can't hurt to at least look. Shelters are easily accessible because you can always just stop in to see the dogs without having any commitment just yet. Some people choose a dog simply based on a photo and short description on the shelter's website, but seeing the dogs in person can make it much easier to see what the dog's personality is like. Also, sometimes shelters have a hard time keeping their websites completely up to date, so there might be some new dogs in the shelter that have not yet been posted online.

Shelters don't always have a huge variety of dogs because each one only has a certain amount of space at a time. Shih Tzu are not commonly found in shelters due to their popularity, but it can't hurt to check. If you happen to come across a dog that you're interested in at a shelter, you can ask to meet them to see how the dog reacts around you specifically.

When meeting a dog at a shelter, they will usually give you all the information known about the dog and let you have some time alone with them in a separate room. This will allow you time to see how the dog acts and will help you decide if this is a dog that will be able to bond with you. Some dogs will be friendly toward you immediately, but others may take time to adjust. If the dog you're meeting with doesn't come running to you right away, that doesn't necessarily mean that the dog dislikes you. Shelters can be scary for dogs, so the first time they meet a potential owner can make them anxious, so remember to be patient with certain dogs.

Before deciding to take a shelter dog home, it is a good idea to have any kids or other dogs in your household meet the dog first. Not all dogs act the same toward children and other pets, so this will be a good way

20

to transition the dog into their new living situation. It is a good idea to spend as much time with the dog as possible before deciding whether or not they are the right fit for you. If there is more than one dog that you're interested in at a shelter, don't be afraid to meet with both of them. You don't need to settle for the first dog you see.

Adopting from a Rescue

While adopting from a shelter is generally easier and cheaper than adopting from a rescue, it is still a good idea to explore both options. Rescues can be more beneficial because there are lots of different rescues to choose from and they typically have a wider selection of dogs than a shelter would. Some rescues focus specifically on smaller dogs or non-shedding dogs, which could help you narrow down your search a lot. The easiest way to find the perfect rescue dog, though, is to simply search online to find all the adoptable dogs in the area.

Rescue dogs are typically found at foster homes, which are just fellow dog lovers who have volunteered to watch the dogs until they have found a home. Once you find a dog that you're interested in, you will be able to talk to the foster parents to schedule a time to meet the dog. This requires more coordination than meeting with a shelter dog, but meeting with the foster parents of a dog can sometimes make the experience more personal. Also, if the dog you're meeting with is not the right fit for you, the foster home can give you suggestions about similar dogs in their rescue. They also might know about dogs that have not been posted online yet and can tell you if any of those new dogs might be a good fit for you.

The process for adopting a rescue often takes longer than from a breeder or shelter because they want to ensure that all their dogs go to a good home. Not every dog rescue is the same, but many of them will want to interview you and your family ahead of time and they may even require a home visit. While this may seem a bit tedious, it shows that the rescue truly cares about their dogs and what happens to them after they are adopted. Plus, if you ever decide to adopt from them again in the future, they will be more than happy to help you find another dog that fits your family well.

Similar to adopting from a shelter, it is important to remember that the first dog you look at isn't always going to be the perfect dog for you. During the process, keep an open mind and don't be afraid to meet with as many dogs as possible. The more dogs you meet, the more likely you are to find the one ideal dog for you. Finding the perfect dog should not be a rushed process by any means, so remember to be patient while looking for your Shih Tzu.

CHAPTER 3
Preparing Your Home for Your Shih Tzu

Once you begin the search for a new dog, prepare your house ahead of time. If you are not used to having a dog in your home, there may be things about your home that need to be adjusted to be more comfortable and safe for your furry friend. It is important that your dog has plenty of space and supplies ready to welcome them during their first day home.

Preparing Space for Your Dog

"Pick up anything and everything off of the floor. Puppies are like vacuum cleaners, and will eat and chew on anything. Have a designated "safe" space for the puppy. I recommend at least one playpen set up so that the puppy will have a safe space to sleep, eat, and play."

Twila Severance
Divine Design Shih Tzu

When you bring your Shih Tzu home, it is normal for you to want to spend as much time with them as possible, but you need to remember that it may take them a while to adjust. They could be playful and energetic at first, but if they prefer to keep to themselves while they get comfortable, then you need to respect that too.

No matter how close you become to your new dog, every Shih Tzu will need some occasional alone time. Therefore, make sure they have a space in the house that is specifically for them. This could simply be a crate with some comfortable bedding in it or a corner of the house to keep some of their toys and supplies. Just an area that they can retreat to if they need to be by themselves for a little bit. Having their own area of the house will help them to feel more at home quicker.

Since Shih Tzu do not need a ton of space to run around inside, you do not need to have a big house to own one. They are typically content with whatever space they are given, no matter how large or small the house may be. Since they are a small, more relaxed breed, they make good apartment dogs—but they'll need to be trained not to bark too of-

Photo Courtesy of
Brittaney Rosenmayer

ten. As long as your Shih Tzu has a designated place to lie down and a window to look out of then they should be more than happy with their living situation.

Larger, more active dogs typically require a fenced in yard or a large outdoor area to run around in, but for a Shih Tzu, that is not necessary. They enjoy exploring outside, but do not need a designated outdoor area. If you live in an apartment or a house with a small yard, you can always take them to the dog park occasionally if you feel that they need more space outside. Otherwise, if you have a porch or patio, your Shih Tzu may enjoy simply sitting out there and admiring the sights. This way they can be lazy and enjoy the outdoors all at once.

Adjusting Current Pets and Children

Even if your Shih Tzu is typically good around children and other dogs, it is still a good idea to slowly introduce them to these other family members. It can be a bit overwhelming for them to have a bunch of un-familiar kids and dogs running at them all at once. If there are multiple kids and pets in your household, introduce them to your new dog one at a time. This can help make the process more comfortable for your new family member. Meeting all of them at once can be a bit scary, especially if the kids and other dogs have a lot of energy.

If there are children in the household, they likely have already met the new dog ahead of time, but it is still a good idea to be careful, espe-cially with younger kids. Children often have a hard time understanding the boundaries of a new dog and will constantly follow them and give more love and affection than the dog really wants. Shih Tzu can become startled if a kid with too much energy comes running toward them or won't leave them alone. Remind children to be gentle around their new family member. Make sure the kids don't smother your new Shih Tzu with too much attention. This will help your new dog to become more comfortable around all family members.

Kids often do not understand a dog's warning signs and this is why they can sometimes get hurt. Make sure to teach kids how to properly treat their dog and how to tell if their dog wants to be left alone. Even sim-ply petting a dog can go wrong, so remember to advise kids to keep their hands away from the dog's face to avoid accidentally startling the dog or poking them in the eye. Shih Tzu often dislike their feet being touched too, so if you notice a child messing with your Shih Tzu's paws, please warn them so they can learn.

If a Shih Tzu dislikes the way kids are acting or if their energy be-comes overwhelming, they may snarl or growl. This is not to be mean and aggressive, but instead to warn others that they are upset or un-comfortable. Make sure kids know that a snarl is a cue to back off. That way, the kids will be able to avoid upsetting the dog, making it easier for them to bond.

Another way to help your dog bond better with your children is to al-low the kids to help you train the dog. Dogs typically will not listen to kids as well as they would adults, so try to show your dog that they should see the kids as equals to you. Training a dog together can also help the dog to grow closer to the entire family in general.

When it comes to other pets, it can be difficult for them to understand that they need to be careful around their new friend. If there is more than

Photo Courtesy of
Mallory Duffy

one dog, introduce them one at a time and allow them enough time to sniff each other. If a dog becomes too playful at first, some Shih Tzu will become uneasy and may snarl or snap at your other dogs. This does not mean that they dislike each other, but it may take your Shih Tzu a bit to become comfortable with these new dogs. Once your Shih Tzu has spent some time around the other dogs, the Shih Tzu will no longer react negatively toward them. Not all Shih Tzu will want to become best friends with other dogs, but over time they will learn to at least tolerate them.

If there are cats in the house, keep an eye on your Shih Tzu when they are around them. Shih Tzu tend to be fairly curious, which can be scary for the cats. The new dog might try to follow the cats around to smell them, but try to teach your Shih Tzu to leave the cats alone. Dogs typically do not understand why cats don't want to smell them and play with them and will be unhappy when the cat finally claws and hisses at them in response.

Photo Courtesy of
Kelly Wallace

Dangerous Things to Look Out For

"Try to have everything ready before the puppy arrives. If there are dangerous power cords or hazards such as a puppy tripping and knocking over a table lamp, those items should be secured, removed, or in the case of power cords, wrapped with material that will help prevent electrocution if chewed."

Twila Severance
Divine Design Shih Tzu

When there's a dog in the house, it is important to never leave food unattended. Even though Shih Tzu are much shorter than most dogs, they can gain an extra skip in their step if they see food sitting out. Keep any food or substances that you don't want your dog getting a hold of far out of reach from them because many human foods can be harmful to dogs, such as grapes and chocolate.

Compared to other breeds, Shih Tzu are not heavy chewers. They may occasionally rip apart something you don't want them to, but they are not likely to destroy the whole house when you're not looking. However, if you do have any problems with chewing, you can buy specific toys so they can have something to chew on. If toys do not interest them, you can always buy them different edible chews to keep them occupied such as bully sticks or antlers. If something has an exciting flavor to it, they will be much more interested in chewing that than any shoes or pillows.

Dogs can be very curious when in a new location, so it is important to keep an eye on your pet when they first explore their new home. If there are specific rooms or areas of the house that you want to keep your dog out of, leave the door closed or put a gate in the way to keep them out. At first, your dog may whine and wonder what's behind the mysterious door, but after a while they will gradually lose interest.

One thing to keep an eye out for is kitty litter. If there is a cat in the house, there is a good chance that your Shih Tzu will try to eat the kitty litter. As disgusting as it is, this is a difficult habit to stop. So, if you cannot seem to teach your Shih Tzu to stay away, you can buy a door strap for whatever room the kitty litter is in. This way, the door will be able to open just wide enough for a cat to slip through, but a Shih Tzu will not be able to squeeze their way in.

Pet Supplies to Purchase

Before bringing your Shih Tzu home, it is important to have all of the basic supplies ready ahead of time. It can be difficult to know your dog's preferences on certain toys and treats, so you can wait until your dog actually arrives to buy more of the extra supplies. Just make sure to have necessities such as a leash and some dog food.

No matter where you get your dog from, there is likely already a certain kind of food that they are eating. Rescues and breeders will inform you about their food brand when you purchase your dog. If the food brand that your dog is used to is not the same brand you'd prefer to give them, you can switch it, but be careful. Try gradually switching the foods by mixing them together for a few days before giving your dog only the new food. This will help to ensure that the sudden change in food does not upset your dog's stomach. If you are unsure which brand of food is best for your dog, try visiting a small, local pet store because even though they have fewer options, their selection is typically only the healthiest brands. They can also help give you advice on which food will benefit your dog best.

When picking out a leash for your dog, choose a shorter one. The longer the leash, the easier it is for your dog to wander away from you

Photo Courtesy of
Sandy Cobb

and get in the way of other people. A lot of people like the extendable leashes for their dog, but these leashes are more dangerous than the traditional ones because it is harder to control your dog. An extendable leash is also much thinner and can be difficult to see, so it is easy for other people and dogs to trip over it. Extendable leashes have also been known to leave nasty burns on people's legs when their dogs get out of hand. This is why a traditional leash will make walking with your dog much easier.

HELPFUL TIP

There's No Place Like Home

Like very young children, your puppy needs your protection. Begin "puppy proofing" before your new companion comes home. Although Shih Tzu are even-tempered, any puppy will get into mischief. Be proactive by removing household chemicals, electrical cords, and tempting indoor plants. Keep interior doors closed to avoid your puppy falling downstairs or entering rooms that are off-limits. Always err on the side of caution with a new puppy.

Have either a bed or crate ready for your dog so that they have a place to lie down when they need some space. A crate is really only needed if you want to train your new dog to stay in a crate when you're not home. Otherwise, a bed will do just fine as a safe space for your dog. If you do decide to go with a crate, make sure it is big enough for your dog to move around and that it has some padding to keep your dog comfortable.

CHAPTER 4
Bringing Home Your Shih Tzu

When you first bring your new dog home, there will likely be lots of excitement, but remember that the first day may not go as smoothly as you'd hoped. There are many things to prepare ahead of time and lots you can do to ensure your new Shih Tzu feels as at home as possible. Allow plenty of time for them to adjust to their new surroundings and don't rush anything.

Pet Supplies to Have Ready

Before bringing your dog home, you should have already bought all their basic supplies. Have these items sitting out when your Shih Tzu arrives so that they can smell all their new stuff. Once they recognize that these supplies are theirs, it will help them to adjust better.

If you forgot any supplies or if you want to go buy your dog a few extra things, then don't be afraid to take your new dog on a trip to the pet store. This way you can help your dog get used to riding in your car and they can help sniff out the items that most interest them.

If your dog seems uneasy in their new home, you may want to guide them to their area of the house to show them that it is okay to lie in their bed and play with the toys. If there are other pets in the house, you want to make sure that all pets understand that these new items are for your new dog specifically. Otherwise, your Shih Tzu may become scared or anxious if their items have some other dog's scent on them.

Always have a bowl of fresh water out for when your dog gets thirsty. Especially since they may be nervous about their new home, they may pant a lot and need plenty of water to stay hydrated. Even if the dish is full, you want to change the water often to ensure it stays fresh.

Shih Tzu are typically good when walking on a leash, but if your dog for some reason pulls all the time, you will want to get a harness for them to prevent them from choking. It is a good idea to wait to buy a harness until you have your dog with you because this way you can try the different types on to find the best fit. Some harnesses can be tricky and make it hard to estimate size when your dog isn't with you.

*Photo Courtesy of
Kayla Wallace*

Another important supply to get either before or when your dog moves in is a name tag for their collar or harness. Include your dog's name and your contact information on it in case the dog gets lost. People don't usually expect their dogs to run away, but it is better to be safe than sorry. Another way to keep them safe is to get them microchipped as another form of identification if they get lost. What many people don't realize is that it is not uncommon for a Shih Tzu to get stolen due to how friendly they are. If your dog does not have a microchip or tag, they could easily come across a person who will decide to keep them as their own. It is important for you to do everything you can to prevent this from happening.

The First Day Home

"There is always a chance that a new pup or adult may not want to eat when they first arrive. They may be confused and afraid, even if they act happy. It's your job to make sure they eat well. Hypoglycemia can set in fast. I recommend adding a little cut chicken or broth, or cottage cheese to their meals to get them to eat."

Debbie Heuston
Debbie's Darlings

Bringing a new puppy home is a lot like bringing home a baby or a toddler. There will be so many new sights, sounds, and smells for your new puppy as well as for an older dog, which may cause them to not want to listen to you at first. You want to make sure everything is dog-proof to help keep your new dog out of trouble. You also want to be gentle and cautious around your new family member. This means that you should talk softly and slowly to your little Shih Tzu, just like you would with a child to help get them to feel safe around you.

Photo Courtesy of Cathy Panuelos

When you first bring your dog home, they will either be extremely excited, extremely nervous, or a mixture of both. As much as you want the first day home to go perfectly, you need to remember that your dog will need some time to adjust. Don't put too much pressure on the idea of your dog fitting in right away.

Remember to pick up any unwanted objects off the floor before bringing your Shih Tzu home. As a puppy, they may want to chew on everything in sight, so it would not be good for your Shih Tzu's first experience home to have them accidentally choke on something. You want to ensure that everything is out of reach from your puppy or new dog when they come home to make sure that they don't get too curious when exploring the house.

Even after being introduced to their new home and new supplies, your dog might still seem a bit unsure of it all. Give your dog some space after a while so they can explore the house for themselves. They will likely just need an extra chance to sniff all the areas and look out all the windows. While they are exploring, keep checking on them to make sure they are staying out of trouble.

In the house, be consistent with your rules and boundaries for your new dog. If you do not want them in certain rooms or on certain furniture, make those commands clear. Don't allow them on the couch at first and then later scold them for being on the couch. These discrepancies in your orders can easily confuse them and make it harder for them to learn your expectations.

HELPFUL TIP
Be Prepared

Before bringing home your new Shih Tzu puppy, prepare for his arrival. Your veterinarian will be your best source for good advice regarding the perfect food for your Shih Tzu. Quality dog food should be provided for your new pet in stainless- steel bowls that are not too deep. Your Shih Tzu will do well to have a slightly elevated bowl to allow better access to food and water. Take the time to shop for an orthopedic, memory foam bed that will support your dog comfortably. Since Shih Tzu may be prone to hip and joint problems, the choice of bed will prove important over time.

A harness is the best choice for your Shih Tzu. As they grow, purchase new harnesses to provide comfort and safety. Talk to your vet about a microchip for your new dog. Update your contact information on the microchip website to allow access if your dog should be lost or stolen.

Taking your new dog for a few walks outside can help them as well. They can sniff the scents of all the neighbor dogs as well as leave their own scent. Walking may be able to distract them from all of the other changes. Shih Tzu typically enjoy smelling new scents outside, so sometimes a walk is all they need to cheer up a bit.

During the first few days home, keep things as normal to your daily routine as possible. A party or big group of people may scare your dog and you don't want them to think that is what it will always be like in their new home. Try to keep things as easygoing as possible until your Shih Tzu has time to adjust.

Photo Courtesy of
Stacey Hughes

The First Night

Dogs typically sleep on and off throughout the day, so when you go to bed, they may not understand that they need to sleep through the whole night. If they sleep in bed with you, you may want to close the door to your bedroom so if they do wake up, they're not wandering around the whole house. If you are a light sleeper, you may wake up every time your Shih Tzu does, but don't worry, over time your dog will slowly begin to adapt to your sleep schedule.

Deciding where your dog sleeps is entirely up to you, but if you are worried about your dog wandering around at night, even just in your room, you may want them to sleep in their crate or a sectioned off area of the house. This can help them to calm down and keep them in one place throughout the night. They may bark at first, but if you let them bark for a little while, they should eventually stop and realize that this is the time to sleep. However, many owners simply prefer to let their Shih Tzu sleep in bed with them since they are a small breed and do not take up much space.

If you have a puppy, they may not be able to hold their bladder throughout the entire night. If you hear your puppy whining in the middle of the night, instead of telling them to be quiet, try taking them out to make sure they don't have an accident. As your Shih Tzu grows older, they should be able to hold it longer, allowing you to actually sleep through the whole night. However, be prepared to lose a little sleep the first few nights as your dog gets used to their new sleeping area.

Choosing a Vet

Because Shih Tzu are a common breed, all vets will likely have some experience working with them. However, you may want to visit the different vets in the area ahead of time to help decide which one would be the best fit for you. They will be able to answer any questions you have about vet visits and health ahead of time.

When you bring your new dog home, the breeder or rescue should have them as healthy as possible, but if you are unsure about your new dog's health, you can always schedule an appointment yourself. This way you can become familiar with your dog's vet and be given any health information that you may need for your new pet.

Your dog's first vet visit will likely be a scary experience for them. While vets are kind and will give your dog treats to calm them down,

Photo Courtesy of
Madison Taylor

there are still a lot of unusual smells at a vet's office for your dog. Especially if they are a puppy, they will not want to sit still during their checkup, but it is important to remain calm and give your dog plenty of love and attention while at the vet so that they will be less worried. Reward them if they behave well during the checkup. Over time, the vet should become less frightening to your dog, making visits to the vet much easier.

To help make the process even easier for your dog, take them for car rides more often than just to the vet. Drive them to the park once in a while because otherwise they will only associate car rides with a negative result, making them resist even going into the car.

If the vet tells you that your new puppy happens to have some type of condition or disease, then this can become an issue. Shih Tzu breeder Joel Clark, from Puppy Love Shih Tzu, states that "if genetic, the breeder needs to know so that they don't sell any more puppies from that mating pair." Even if you had a great experience with your breeder, it is important to notify them if something went wrong in your dog's genetics. Doing this will prevent future dog owners from getting the same unwanted conditions and traits in their future puppy.

Obedience Classes

Obedience classes are not for everyone, but it can't hurt to give them a try if you need help training your dog. Since Shih Tzu are a stubborn breed, it may be difficult to get them to listen to you, so a professional class or trainer may benefit your dog.

Photo Courtesy of Alicia Cesana

If you adopt your dog from a rescue, they will typically have recommendations on helpful classes for your specific dog. Some shelters also hold their own classes at the location. Vets, groomers, and local pet stores will usually be able to give you good suggestions as well. Otherwise, you can simply search for obedience classes online, but you may find a wide variety.

Classes can benefit you and your pup because they can help the two of you to bond. The classes should be able to help get your dog to listen to you more often. They will also help your dog to be more well behaved overall and have better manners on a day-to-day basis.

Obedience classes can be pricey, but the cost varies based on the class you choose. More stubborn dogs such as Shih Tzu may need to take classes longer to be properly trained. Even though classes will take extra time out of your day, they could benefit your dog greatly, especially if it's a puppy. If you feel that you can train your dog just as well on your own, then classes may not even be necessary. The decision is completely up to you and what you think is best for your dog.

CHAPTER 5
Basic Training

"There is always a chance that a new pup or adult may not want to eat when they first arrive. They may be confused and afraid, even if they act happy. It's your job to make sure they eat well. Hypoglycemia can set in fast. I recommend adding a little cut chicken or broth, or cottage cheese to their meals to get them to eat."

Debbie Heuston
Debbie's Darlings

Photo Courtesy of
Kate Wieser

Whether you have an adult dog or a newborn puppy, every pet will need some type of training to adjust to a new lifestyle. A puppy will need to learn the basic commands while a full-grown dog may just need to learn how to listen to you specifically. Either way, it is important to remain patient with your new dog and give them time to learn what you expect from them.

It is important to remember that the most important part of training any dog is consistency and repetition. If you keep trying the same commands and lessons over and over again, then eventually your dog will catch on. Try to develop a specific schedule for training so that your puppy can get in the habit of listening to you and training often. Just remember to try your best not to lose your patience during any part of the training process.

Housetraining

"Consistency is the best thing. Keeping them confined in small areas is the best thing especially when you can't watch them, even when they seem to be doing really well. They may be doing really well for a while but when they start teething they will usually start having some house training issues again."

Lisa McKinney
Mr. Foo's Shih Tzu

If you adopted an adult dog, then they are likely already house-trained, but if you have a puppy then this is an essential part of the training process. Right away, you want to teach your puppy that if they need to relieve themselves, then they should go to the bathroom outside. This is a part of training that may take the most time and effort. It can be easy to become frustrated if you can't get your puppy to listen, so if things don't go as planned, just take a deep breath and keep trying.

The younger the puppy is, the harder it is for them to hold it. Take them outside as much as possible to avoid accidents. Stefanie Marie Peacock, a certified Shih Tzu breeder from Peacock Shih Tzu Puppies, states that you should "remember that your puppy will not have complete control of their bladder until they are 5-7 months old." This means that if you have a puppy, they should be taken out every few hours until they can learn to control when they need to use the bathroom. Expect a lot of long nights at first because your puppy will likely need to go at some point while you're trying to sleep as well.

Adult dogs can hold it in for much longer, but that doesn't mean you should expect them to. Regardless of how old your dog is, you should still take them outside quite a bit. It can be boring for a dog to be cooped up inside all day, especially when there are so many interesting smells for them outside. Don't limit their walks or bathroom times simply because you don't feel like it. Your dog's life shouldn't always be planned around your needs because they also have their own needs to worry about. Therefore, give your dog plenty of time outside each day.

The most important times to take your dog outside are right when you wake up and right before you go to bed. This can help your dog sleep through the night without having to get up to pee. Don't take your puppy outside at night and then stay up for a while before going to bed or wake up in the morning and get ready before letting them outside. The

longer they have to hold it in overnight, the more uncomfortable it will be for them.

When you're potty training your dog, it is a good idea to take them to the same spot each time. At this spot, make sure you are only there until they pee. Don't play with them while you are in that area or they may think of it as a play area rather than a potty area. Be consistent so they can learn the routine of going to the bathroom in this area outside.

While a puppy is learning, they will have the occasional accident. It just happens. If you catch them in the act, then make a loud sound to startle them so that they understand what they're doing is wrong. Then take them outside immediately so they can relieve themselves where they're supposed to. However, if you catch an accident after it has already happened, then scolding your dog is not the best solution. A puppy cannot understand what they did wrong if you punish them for an act that has already happened. They will only get it if they are scolded while they are doing it. The best thing to do is simply clean up the mess and keep a close eye on them to make sure you catch them if they attempt to do it again.

Every time your dog goes to the bathroom outside, give them a small treat right away. This will help them to associate going to the bathroom outside with a good experience and help show them that outside is where they are supposed to go. Once they seem to be getting the hang of it, you can substitute treats for praise and attention.

If you have your own fenced in backyard, then it may be a good idea to get a doggy door leading out into your yard. This way, if your dog needs to relieve themselves, then they can learn to let themselves out, which can be easier for them to learn. At first, they may not be able to make it past the porch, but at least their accident will still be outside rather than on the carpet or tile floor.

When your puppy is being housetrained, it is important to wipe your dog's butt after each time they go number two. If you do not do so, their feces can get stuck to them and become hard as a rock over time. If this happens, they may not be able to go to the bathroom after a while or it will become painful for them each time they poop. This can cause a hernia or other medical issues, so if this somehow happens to your puppy, you must visit the vet right away to ensure that the issue does not get any worse.

*Photo Courtesy of
Sara Reilly*

Crate Training

When leaving your dog alone, it is common to worry about them having accidents or getting into trouble, which is why many owners lean toward crate training. Using a crate is not necessary and many Shih Tzu don't need it, but you might feel more comfortable using one at least until your dog becomes completely comfortable in your home. This way, you know they will not get into anything that you don't want them to. After you've had your Shih Tzu for a while, you can try leaving them outside of the crate because most likely, they will just sleep while you're gone. However, if you decide to use a crate, don't keep your dog in it for long periods of time often, especially if they are a puppy. They need time to adjust to being in the crate. Sticking them in there all day at first would be way too much for them to handle and not really fair to your new dog at all.

When selecting a crate, you will need to buy one that is big enough for your dog to comfortably fit into, but not so big that they can freely walk around in it. This is because if they have too much space, they could easily have an accident in one corner and then just lie on the other side of the crate with no worries. Even if you are worried about your dog having an accident in the crate though, you should still keep a comfortable blanket or bedding in the bottom of the crate. Otherwise, it will be uncomfortable for your dog to sit on the hard, plastic bottom for long periods of time. If you are worried about them getting the blanket dirty, you can add a layer of newspapers or towels to help clean it up easier. Just remember that blankets are washable, so if anything happens while you're gone, there is no need to freak out at your dog.

Crate training can be a good way to help housetrain your puppy as well because be-

HELPFUL TIP
Crate Training

Breeders and veterinarians often suggest using a crate for puppies and older dogs. The crate should never be utilized for punishment but should be thought of as a safe den for your dog. Choose a crate that is large enough for your dog to sit, stand, and turn around in with ease and comfort. The crate should be kept in the main area of the home where the family spends most of its time. Beside a soft, warm bottom liner or pad, you should add a small water dish and toys to your dog's crate. The enclosure should never be used as a punishment because the dog will associate it with a feeling of chastisement. You want your dog to enter the crate willingly, for times when you leave the house, go to sleep for the night, or are doing chores around the house.

ing in the crate will help teach them not to go to the bathroom while they're inside. It is uncomfortable for a dog to have an accident and then have to lie in it afterward, so this will make them try their hardest to hold it while they are in their crate. However, many Shih Tzu breeders suggest that instead of using a crate to housetrain your pup, try a fenced in area of the house with potty pads in it. This will give your dog more space to run around. Also, sometimes, if a dog has an accident in their crate too often, they could become used to being dirty, which would make the training harder. Therefore, you may want to consider a pen or gate as a better way to contain your dog when you're not around.

While the crate is usually just an easy way to keep your dog contained at night or while you're gone, it should also be used as a safe space for your dog. You don't want them to be upset every time you make them go into the crate. Reward them when they go into the crate on command, so they associate it with a good result. Even if they are hesitant at first, Shih Tzu are usually fine with being in it because it is just another place for them to sleep. Even when you are home, keep the door to the crate open in case your dog just feels like lying in it from time to time. If trained properly, your dog will enjoy this space instead of fear it.

An important part of crate training that many dog owners forget is that the crate should never be used as a punishment. If your dog chews up your shoes or has an accident, you should not shove them into the crate to teach them a lesson. This will only scare them and make them want to stay as far away from the crate as possible. If you use it for negative reasons, they will think they are being punished every time you go somewhere and leave them behind in that crate.

Chewing

Shih Tzu are not a breed that chews a lot, but all puppies can go through a teething phase, so try to keep valuable objects out of reach. If you notice your dog is chewing on unwanted objects too often, you can purchase plenty of different bones and toys for them to chew on instead. This will help to teach them what is okay to chew on and what isn't. If you catch them chewing on something that they're not supposed to, scold them and then give them a toy or chew instead. When you visit a pet store, you can ask them about what types of chews they specifically recommend for Shih Tzu.

According to Shih Tzu breeder Stefanie Marie Peacock, "The teeth that your baby has when you adopt them from me, they will lose them all and have a full new set within 4-6 months of age." This means that until your Shih Tzu is six months old, you need to expect them to chew a lot. Most dogs love to chew on wood, so watch out for table and chair legs. If your dog does sink their teeth into some of your furniture, try not to get upset with them. It is just part of their teething process to help ease the pain. Just keep a close eye on them and keep plenty of toys lying around for them to chew on and you should be good.

It is likely that your dog will get a hold of something they're not supposed to at some point. You may think everything is out of reach, but you really never know when your dog could sneak around and somehow get a hold of something toxic. To ensure that your dog never suffers from any type of food poisoning or other sudden conditions, it is a good idea to keep the number of the vet, emergency clinic, and Animal Poison Control Center nearby so that you can quickly call one of them if an emergency occurs. It is always better to be safe than sorry.

Growling and Barking

As many small dogs are, Shih Tzu can be known as a bit of a yippy breed. Even if they don't bark often, once they start barking, it can be difficult to get them to stop. More specifically, Shih Tzu typically bark when they see other dogs walk by or come near them. This is an important behavior to stop because if you allow them to growl and bark at other dogs, then your dog might think it is okay to be aggressive toward these other pets.

Every time your Shih Tzu starts to growl or bark at another dog, give them a command to make them stop. Make sure this command is consistent every time so that they can associate the command with their actions. If you notice your Shih Tzu spot another dog and they do not make an attempt to growl or bark, award them or give them praise to encourage them to keep up that behavior.

If your dog is a rescue dog that already has a bad habit of barking, then it may be more difficult to properly train them to correct this behavior. Sometimes they simply will not listen to your commands and continue barking every time they cross paths with another dog. If this is the case, then you need to find a way to show your dog that you are the boss and not them. An easy way to do this is if you catch them barking or growling, you can simply grab on tightly to the hair on their face and tell them no and this will usually get them to stop. It will not harm your dog in any way, but it will typically get them to realize that you are serious with your commands. Even if it does not get them to stop barking right away, it should cause them to bark less often. You never want your dog to think that they are in control or they will try to get away with as many things as possible.

The more your Shih Tzu is around other dogs, the less likely they are to bark at them. Therefore, make an effort to socialize your pup as much as possible.

Digging

Some Shih Tzu are compelled to dig holes, but many owners frown upon this because it makes them extremely dirty. Also, if they try digging in the neighbor's yards or on public property, this could easily become a problem. Despite how small the breed is, they can dig a hole surprisingly fast. Therefore, as soon as you see your dog start to crouch down to dig, immediately command them to stop.

The easiest way to stop your dog from digging in unwanted areas is to keep them distracted with other things. Bring toys for them to play with or treats to draw them away from the hole. If your dog realizes that they can get a toy or a treat instead of digging, they will quickly lose interest in this bad behavior and want to play with you instead.

Separation Anxiety

Shih Tzu can become very attached to their owners and become upset the second they are left alone. You can't be with your dog every second of every day, so you need to find a way to make their alone time easier for them. For example, you can make sure your dirty laundry is accessible to them while you're gone. Oftentimes they will want to lie in it because it smells strongly like you. If you don't like the idea of having your laundry sitting out, then there are dog beds that you can purchase that are made specifically for stuffing with your laundry to help with your dog's separation anxiety.

If you ever have to leave your dog with someone else for a little while, bring something that smells like you, such as a blanket or pillow. This way they will still be able to smell you and they know that you will be coming back for them. This will help make their time away from you a little less scary.

Photo Courtesy of
Lori Gearheart

Running Away

Many people assume that their dog is too well behaved and too attached to them to ever run away. In some cases, this may be true, but sometimes dogs can get lost and have difficulty finding their way home. They could just harmlessly wander off in the wrong direction and not remember how to get back home. Whatever the case, it is important to keep an eye on your dog and help teach them not to run away.

For the most part, you should always keep your dog on a leash outside. If they are at the dog park or another fenced in area, that can be an exception, but otherwise, even if you're just walking around your neighborhood, your dog should be leashed at all times. Even if you have complete trust in your dog, you never know what could happen, especially with a dog that is newer to your house because they may not know where home is just yet.

You should also keep a tag with your contact information on your dog at all times. This way, if they ever are without a leash or if they ever happen to wander off, at least someone will know how to contact you when they find your dog. If your dog gets lost without a collar or tag on, anyone that sees your dog will just assume that they're a stray.

Leaving Your Dog Home Alone

Besides separation anxiety, Shih Tzu usually have very few problems with being left alone. Whether they're in a crate or not, they will likely just sleep or look out the window the whole time you're gone.

If you have to be gone most of the day, be sure to spend plenty of time with your dog before you leave and after you get home. Give them just as much attention as you would if you were home all day. It is not fair for your dog to get less love just because you're gone more. To help cheer them up, give them a treat or bone to chew on when you leave so they won't be as sad to see you go.

If your Shih Tzu is not used to you leaving just yet, they may bark for a while once you step out the door. If you hear them barking, don't immediately go back in to tell them to stop. If you do, they will think that if they bark, you will come back for them. Instead, let them bark it out for a little bit. If you are worried about disturbing your neighbors, you can always leave and then wait outside until you hear your dog stop barking. This will help to give you peace knowing that your dog is fine and will not bark the entire time. Leaving your dog home alone can be hard on both you and your dog at first, but over time, it will become much more comfortable for the two of you.

CHAPTER 6
Socializing with People and Animals

"I believe it is very important to get you Shih Tzu out in public as much as possible. Once your new puppy is fully vaccinated, take then with you as much as you can. If you live near a dog park, you can take then there to play and socialize."

Mollie Doucette
Tatnicland Shih Tzu

Having your dog get along with you and your family members may be the biggest concern to you at first, but it is also important that your dog gets along with those around you as well. Every dog takes a different amount of time to get used to others, so it is important to find out how comfortable your dog is with different people and animals and teach them to be as social is possible.

Make sure your puppy has received all the required shots before you take them out to meet other dogs. You don't want your dog to catch any diseases and you certainly don't want them spreading them either. While it may seem important to try and socialize your dog as soon as possible, you never want to put anyone at risk, so make sure your puppy has shots before taking them around other animals.

Behavior Around Other Dogs

When getting a new dog, many owners tend to focus primarily on the tricks and training and sort of neglect the social aspect of it. Don't let all of the chaos of getting a new dog distract you from learning your dog's behavior. Paying attention to how your dog reacts to other dogs is one of the most important parts of raising your pup. The younger your dog is when you start teaching them to socialize, then the more well behaved they will likely be.

Shih Tzu may feel the urge to growl when an unfamiliar dog comes near them. For many dogs, they feel comfortable once they get a chance to sniff each other. The more you have your Shih Tzu around other dogs, the more comfortable they will likely become.

However, never force your Shih Tzu to get along with other dogs. Some Shih Tzu just prefer people and that's how they'll always be. If you force them to play with others, they may become annoyed, similar to how you would if someone was constantly forcing you to hang out with other people. It may take some time to learn how your dog feels about other dogs.

Shih Tzu typically prefer smaller dogs over bigger ones. Large dogs can sometimes be too much for a smaller dog to handle and can be intimidating at first. This isn't true for all Shih Tzu though, because sometimes this breed likes to think that they're bigger than they actually are, which means they will try to boss bigger dogs around. If your Shih Tzu does this, don't pick them up to take them away from the big dog. This is because when you pick up your dog, they will feel like they are bigger and more superior than the other dog and this will not help their dominant behaviors at all.

Take socializing with other dogs slowly. Some Shih Tzu will befriend other dogs immediately while others might not even want other dogs to sniff them. This is true for any breed, so even if your Shih Tzu is good around other dogs, you might still want to be careful. If your Shih Tzu approaches a dog that dislikes other pets, then they my snap and scare your dog. Don't get mad if a dog dislikes your dog. Every dog has a different personality and different attitude toward other dogs, so respect that just as you would expect other people to with your dog.

HELPFUL TIP
Joining the Pack

Shih Tzu get along well with people and other dogs if socialized early and often. They are normally not aggressive with other dogs, enjoying the company of animals and humans. Although they are naturally sweet and gentle dogs, they must be trained well to avoid "little dog syndrome."

Some pet parents decide to add another dog to their pack as a companion for their existing pet. Often, pet owners do not realize that a second pet is twice the work and twice the expense. Know the commitment you are taking on before you fall in love with your new pet.

Care must be taken when introducing the new dog to the "pack" and "den." There will be an existing hierarchy in the household and a clear leader in place. The older dog will take time to allow the new pet to enter the pack. Sometimes, the first dog will correct the puppy when it crosses the line. Owners need to be diligent and watchful to ensure this behavior is done in a safe way. If the behavior becomes dangerous, consult a professional trainer. Try to anticipate problems to avoid negative interaction. Supply separate water and food dishes for your dogs. Each animal should be given a bed, toys, and designated space in the house. Over time, and with patience, your four-legged family members will enjoy the companionship.

49

Ways to Socialize Your Dog with Other Pets

"I believe it is very important to get you Shih Tzu out in public as much as possible. Once your new puppy is fully vaccinated, take then with you as much as you can. If you live near a dog park, you can take then there to play and socialize."

Mollie Doucette
Tatnicland Shih Tzu

Getting a new dog is exciting, so you'll likely want to take your pup as many places at possible. However, being out in public a lot can be scary for a new dog, especially a puppy. There are lots of unfamiliar sounds and noises. It doesn't have to be scary, though. Socialization is important in a dog's life so that they can get used to these types of changes.

Take your dog for walks often, not only as exercise, but also to social-ize them. This way, they will likely run into other dogs while you are walk-ing, which can help them to become more comfortable with other pets around them. If they want to go toward another dog, allow them to sniff each other, but hold on tightly to their leash in case your dog becomes aggressive. This way, even if your Shih Tzu dislikes the other dog, you can still have control of them with the leash. Some Shih Tzu can be stubborn when their owner tries to drag them away from another dog, so if this is the case, then you can get a harness for your dog to better control them and to avoid choking them when you pull.

Once you feel that your dog is improving their socialization with oth-er pets, you can take them to the dog park or another public area every so often. This way they can meet a greater variety of dogs rather than just the same few neighbor dogs over and over again. This will also give them more space to run free. If you are concerned about how your dog will act, you can keep them on their leash at first to see how they react to this new environment. However, you should at least give them a chance to roam free and see how they behave around others after a little while. It wouldn't be fair for the other dogs to get to run around freely at the park while your dog remains tied up the whole time.

If you ever take your dog to a friend's house and they have pets, al-low the two pets to meet right away to help make your visit more com-fortable. If you just come over and your dog unexpectedly meets the oth-er dog, they could end up fighting or freaking out. You need to show your dog that this other pet is a friend. However, your Shih Tzu will get jealous if you pet a friend's dog more than you pet them, so make sure to still give your dog just as much love as usual.

Photo Courtesy of
Teresa Brown

Properly Greeting New People

HELPFUL TIP
Socialization

Although Shih Tzu are even-tempered and affable dogs, when they are not properly socialized they may become anxious. Anxiety may lead to excessive barking, jumping up, or chewing episodes. They get very attached to their owners and may suffer separation anxiety. The first months of a puppy's life are the most important time for socialization. Introduce your new friend to children, adults, and other animals as often as possible. Take him with you to the park, on walks, to the pet store, and dog parks. Although this socialization is purposeful from your perspective, it is enjoyable for your Shih Tzu.

When you get your new dog, all of your friends and family are likely going to want to meet your new family member as soon as possible. While it is good to expose your dog to new people, you don't want to invite everyone over at once. Too many people can be overwhelming for your Shih Tzu and since they are small, they may become scared of being stepped on with all the extra feet around.

Therefore, try to schedule only one or two people meeting your new Shih Tzu at a time. This way, your dog can have some one-on-one time with each friend, which will help them to form a bond with each person. This will also help them to be less scared next time those people come to visit because when they smell them, they may recognize them.

When you walk your dog, people will likely stop to ask if they can pet your dog. These can be good opportunities to help get your dog used to being around unfamiliar people. Many Shih Tzu love any chance they can to be petted, but if someone asks to pet your dog and you feel hesitant, don't feel bad saying no. You don't want to socialize your dog too much at once if they are clearly not comfortable with it yet.

Shih Tzu Around Children

No matter where you go, children will always want to pet your cute little dog. Kids get excited to see small dogs and may approach your dog without even asking first. You do not need to deny children petting privileges of your dog, but remind each kid to be gentle with your Shih Tzu. If you notice your Shih Tzu trying to escape a child's grasp, jump in and take your dog away from the kid as quickly as possible to avoid any possible growling or snapping from your pet.

Photo Courtesy of Brittaney Rosenmayer

Kids will often want to pick up your small dog too, but this is a bad idea because if they accidentally drop them, that can be a traumatizing experience for your pet. If you do allow a kid to hold your pup, show them the correct way to hold a small dog and stand right beside them while they have the dog in their arms. Make sure they keep one arm under the dog's butt so the Shih Tzu doesn't slide out of their arms. This can help to protect your dog as well as any small dogs the child may try to hold in the future.

CHAPTER 7
Exercise

S hih Tzu are not the most active dog breed, but every dog needs at least some exercise, both physically and mentally. It is important to try challenging your Shih Tzu a little from time to time, but don't work them too hard. They enjoy their lazy time more than most dogs would, but it is good to remember that every Shih Tzu has different requirements and different needs.

Exercise Requirements

HELPFUL TIP
Exercise

Although Shih Tzu are not high-energy dogs, they shouldn't be considered lazy. Regular exercise not only helps with socialization, it helps to strengthen circulation and encourage respiratory health. Regular 20-30 minute walks twice a day, or more will improve digestion and encourage restful sleep habits. The playful Shih Tzu is a light to moderate chewer who will enjoy puzzle toys that have hidden, healthy treats. An active Shih Tzu will provide you with years of loyal companionship.

While Shih Tzu do not require any jogging or agility course–type exercise, they do need to occasionally get out of the house and stop being lazy for a while. At least a walk each day is usually needed for a Shih Tzu, but it really depends on the specific dog. Younger Shih Tzu may want to walk and play as much as possible while an elderly dog may want to avoid being on their feet as much as possible. The more time you spend around your dog, the more you will learn about their exercise needs.

Larger dogs may require a plan when it comes to how much exercise is needed, but with a Shih Tzu, you can be more casual with their workouts. The most important thing to remember is not to let them be overly lazy. If all they do is sleep all day, then they are less likely to stay healthy throughout their life. Don't work them too hard, but be careful that they aren't gaining too much weight.

For most Shih Tzu, a walk a day is more than enough to maintain their energy. Some Shih Tzu may want more than this while others may want to avoid working out altogether. It may take time to see which pace your pup is at, but once you get used to spending time with your dog, you can decide exactly how much exercise they really need.

Photo Courtesy of
Judi Gullickson

Ways to Exercise Your Pup

Walks are the best way to keep your Shih Tzu in shape. They don't have to be long walks, but they certainly need to be more than just quickly taking them outside to do their business. If you have time to spare, let your Shih Tzu keep walking until they seem tired or act like they want to go back home. You want them to get all their energy out while they can so that they aren't anxious when you leave them alone.

While it may be easier to just walk your Shih Tzu around your neighborhood whenever it's convenient, that may not always be the best decision for your dog. Shih Tzu like to experience a variety of different locations. They like to find new smells and chase different critters, but it is difficult for them to do that if they're only walked throughout the same route in your neighborhood every single day. You don't have to take them somewhere new all the time, but every once in a while, try to mix it up and take them to different areas and parks. This will help them to keep up their energy and allow them to get more exercise than they typically would otherwise.

If your dog is not a fan of walks for whatever reason, then there are other exercise options for them. Many Shih Tzu love to play with anything that squeaks, so if you play with your Shih Tzu enough, then it can

Photo Courtesy of Gabriel Perez

actually be good exercise for them. They typically enjoy fetching or playing tug of war with their toys. If these games are played repeatedly, they can tire your dog out and help them be more active. If your dog has a lot of energy and wants to run around playing with you, then don't ignore them. The more you play with them, the better their energy and exercise will likely be.

If it is really hot outside, you may want to avoid long walks that day. With the Shih Tzu's short snout, it can be difficult for them to breathe in the hot weather sometimes. As much as they need some exercise, you do not want them to get heatstroke. Be careful not to work your Shih Tzu too hard.

Cold weather is not the exact same scenario, but Shih Tzu are typically not a fan of the cold. They would much rather be curled up in a blanket than walking around in the snow, as many dog owners would be too. However, you cannot avoid walking your dog all winter. It doesn't need to be as frequent as when it is nice out, but it is good to still take them for the occasional walk even if it is a bit chilly.

Maintaining a Healthy Weight

If you allow your Shih Tzu to be too lazy, then it can be easy for them to gain some extra weight. Shih Tzu tend to have more of a round figure to begin with, but without proper care, they can easily get some extra chunk on top of that. If exercising more is not helping your Shih Tzu's weight, then you likely need to cut back on treats or on food portions. It is hard to resist your dog's cute face, but that doesn't mean you should slip them some food every time they beg. You can visit a local pet store to find some healthier treat options if need be. There are also specific types of dog food specifically designed to manage your dog's weight, so those can also be good to try if you need some help in that area.

If you don't worry about your Shih Tzu's weight while they're young, then it could cost them as they grow older. Overweight dogs are more likely to have joint issues and problems walking as they grow old. Therefore, keep these consequences in mind when thinking about your dog's weight.

Photo Courtesy of
Heather Reid

Keeping Your Shih Tzu Occupied

This breed does not require much mental exercise either. They are typically content with just lying around and looking out the window. However, this does not mean that you should never challenge your dog mentally. Even with little need for mental exercise, your dog will sometimes get bored and want constant attention. Purchase plenty of toys and chews to keep your dog occupied. Buy a large variety so they won't quickly lose interest.

As long as you give your Shih Tzu a good amount of attention, they will always be perfectly occupied. They just need something to do whenever they wake up from a nap, so it is good if you are willing to play with them during this time. If you don't have enough toys for your dog and you don't play with them enough, then they can easily get bored, which could cause them to get into trouble instead. You want to teach your Shih Tzu that playing is much more fun than getting into things they're not supposed to.

CHAPTER 8
Teaching Your Shih Tzu

"Shih Tzu can be stubborn when it comes to training. Even though they are smart they do have a mind of their own, so you need to be firm with them and make training fun so they do not lose interest."

Mollie Doucette
Tatnicland Shih Tzu

As you bond with your new dog, there are many different things that you need to teach them. Some people think of commands as just fun tricks, but they can also help improve your dog's knowledge as well. The more they learn, the smarter and more obedient they will become. Therefore, if you think your dog doesn't need to be taught any more commands, then that may not be the case. Dogs are always excited to learn more.

Where to Practice

You may become set on one specific place to practice training your dog, whether it be because of convenience or space or any other reason. However, if your dog only learns to do commands in one spot, then they may think that that is the only place they need to do those actions. Therefore, try to mix up locations every once in a while, so that your dog is not always practicing in the same place over and over again.

When you're starting to train your dog, you may want to begin in a quieter environment—ideally somewhere inside with few distractions. This will help your dog to focus better at first. Once they seem to be getting the hang of your commands, then you can *Photo Courtesy of Adena Glebus*
move on to more public locations and see if you can still get them to listen even while other things are going on around them.

Clear Expectations

What many owners don't understand when it comes to dog training is that your dog needs to be trained at a level that they can understand. When you command your dog to do something that you have not trained them on, then they will likely be confused and not understand what you want them to do. You will usually need to show them what you are expecting. For example, if you want your dog to go in their crate, show them where to go when you first give the command. This way, they can learn to associate the word you're saying with where you want them to go or what you want them to do. It may take your Shih Tzu a while to understand, so just keep repeating the action and the command often to help them catch on. Some dogs can learn much quicker than others, so don't get frustrated if your dog doesn't pick up on it right away.

Also, when you give commands, remember to be consistent. Don't use two interchangeable words for the same command. Your dog will not be able to understand why you want them to do one thing while saying something else. Keep commands simple and to the point when teaching them to your dog. They learn from repetition, so the more they do a trick, the easier it will be for them to master it.

Primary Reinforcements

HELPFUL TIP
Instructions
and Commands

Certain commands should be taught to all dogs, including your Shih Tzu. The "good boy" command should be one of the first used to train your puppy. Consistent, positive verbal "good boy" commands can be reinforced with healthy treats and well-deserved affection. When training your dog to "come," it is best to have another person to assist you. Your buddy trainer should lightly restrain your dog while you go a safe distance away. When you command the dog to "come," the partner trainer should free the dog to join you. This takes time and patience and should be followed with appropriate praise for your pet. When the dog is consistently performing to this command, you might want to attempt "hide and seek" with your dog in a safe, secure area such as a fenced yard. Your constant and steady training will be rewarded in the long run.

When first training your dog, especially if they are still a young puppy, you will want to use a positive reinforcement that is interesting to your dog. This is typically a small low-calorie treat, but some dogs will prefer a toy or bone to chew on if treats aren't their thing. Don't just pick out any treat though; make sure it is something that really interests your dog because this will help to motivate them better once they realize that every time they correctly follow a command, they get a delicious treat.

Every dog has different preferences when it comes to treats and rewards. Bring your dog to the pet store with you to help select one that smells good to them. Pet stores typically have treats that are specifically made for training. You'll want to make sure the treat is healthy and low in calories for your dog so that they don't suddenly gain a lot of weight from all the training.

Photo Courtesy of
Casey Connolly

Secondary Reinforcements

After a while, you're not going to want to give your dog a treat every single time they do something right. Otherwise, you could end up spending a lot of money on treats and also, too many treats are not good for your dog. Therefore, you can gradually begin introducing secondary reinforcements, like a positive response, such as "good girl" or "good boy," or simply just an extra pat on the head. Some owners like to buy a clicker to reward their dogs too. A clicker makes a little sound that you can teach your dog is a positive sound. Therefore, if they do something right, you can use the clicker and they will recognize that they have been good.

Dangers of Negative Reinforcement

Many people think the best way to get their dogs to learn is to scold them, but that is rarely the case. If you raise your voice or yell at your dog when they do something wrong, all it usually does is scare them because it is hard for them to understand what they did wrong. Even if you yell at them every time they misbehave, they will not understand the correlation and it will not help the training process in any way. So, be careful when you have the urge to scold your pet. Instead, focus more on rewarding good behavior. If a mistake is made, you can just try again.

Some people may think their dog fearing them is a good idea, but just because they get scared when you yell doesn't mean they will learn. If you yell at or scare your dog for going to the bathroom inside, it may not correct that behavior, but instead it will make them realize that they shouldn't have accidents in front of you. This may cause them to sneak off into a different area of the house if they really have to go instead of simply learning to go outside. It is easy to get them to understand things they do right, but when it comes to punishments, it just is not as beneficial as many owners might think.

Owner Behavior

While how your dog reacts is very important in training, how you act toward them also plays a huge role in how they behave. Dogs may not be able to understand specific commands that they are unfamiliar with, but they can tell when you are upset or stressed. This can make it harder for them to listen to you while training if they know that something is wrong.

Photo Courtesy of Mollie Doucette

Even if you've had a rough day, it is important to try to remain cheerful toward your dog. It will help them relax and become more focused. If your dog can tell that you're not happy, they will respond to that instead of paying full attention to your commands.

Shih Tzu can get distracted easily while training, which is a reasonable thing to get frustrated at. However, no matter how upset you get with them, you can't let your anger show. If your dog feels that you are frustrated with them, then this could scare them and make the training process even longer.

Basic Commands

Despite being difficult to train, Shih Tzu can still easily be taught simple commands such as "sit," "stay," and "come." They will usually pick up on these without intense training, but if you want them to learn a greater variety of basic commands, it could take some time. Focus most of your training on one command at a time to help improve the results.

Many people like to use hand motions for basic commands. This way, if you don't want to yell out specific commands in public, you can just show the symbol to command your dog. For example, people typically use a closed fist for "sit" and an outstretched hand for "stay." You do not have to use these exact hand gestures, but make sure every time you give the command, you use the same gesture to avoid confusing your dog.

Your dog likely will not respond to commands and gestures immediately. You may need to help show them what to do, such as lightly touching their back to get them to sit down. Once they do the right action, say the command along with it to help them associate what they did to the command itself. You will need to repeat this lots of times to help your dog to understand the correlation.

It is important to teach your Shih Tzu at least a few basic commands. This way, if you catch them misbehaving, you can tell them to sit or stay to help keep them contained. The better trained they are and the more commands they know, the easier it will be to get them to stop bad habits.

Advanced Commands

More difficult commands such as "roll over" and "shake" are harder for Shih Tzu to understand, but not impossible. You need to have patience if you are interested in teaching them these more advanced tricks. These commands are more for show, but they can also help your pup to become even more obedient.

For these tricks, you may need to teach them in multiple steps. For example, if you want to teach your dog to roll over, then they will need to learn to lie down first. If you want them to shake, they will need to learn to sit on command as well. The more tricks they learn, the more you can add on to them. You can teach them to crawl, spin, or even dance. You never need to stop training your dog, but try not to introduce too many new tricks to your Shih Tzu at once. It may become a bit much for them.

If you spend enough time training your Shih Tzu, they will likely learn to enjoy and become eager to learn more tricks. If you're feeling lucky, you can teach them helpful tricks, such as picking up their toys, opening doors with the help of a rope, and bringing you certain items such as shoes. These complex tricks are typically aimed for larger, more intelligent dogs, but with a certain amount of determination and trust, you can get your Shih Tzu to do them with a good amount of time and effort.

Photo Courtesy of Timothy Johnson

CHAPTER 9
Dealing with Unwanted Behaviors

"Shih Tzu's are known to have separation anxiety. So if left alone for periods of time they display this through some bad behaviors. Things like getting into the garbage, going potty in the house, ect..."

Hiedi Johnson

Even though your dog may be completely perfect in your eyes, there are always certain behaviors that can be fixed or at least improved upon. Sometimes your dog will have bad habits that you have become used to, but then those habits can be harmful or annoying to those around you. Learn to improve your dog's unwanted behaviors as soon as you can to help protect you, your dog, and everyone else who crosses your path.

What Is Bad Behavior in Dogs?

Every dog owner may have a different definition of what a bad behavior may be. A dog's barking may irritate one person while appear adorable to another. Every owner has their different preferences and ways to train their dog. However, when bringing your dog in public, there is usually a certain way that they are expected to act. For Shih Tzu, their most common bad behavior traits are excessive barking, aggressive behavior toward other dogs, and wandering too far away from their owners.

Even if your dog's unideal traits don't bother you, they could be affecting those around you. For example, you might not mind if your dog runs up to another dog, but that owner might prefer that you keep your dog under better control. If someone asks you to keep your dog on a leash or to get them to stop barking, don't get upset. They're usually not trying to be rude, they are typically just looking out for their own dogs and the other dogs around them. Plus, you don't want to be known as the owner with a poorly trained pup. You want to make sure you are in control of your dog at all times.

If you don't have great control over your dog, then they likely will not behave well in public. Your dog may be an angel at home, but that doesn't mean they will act that well everywhere. A different location can be a lot for a dog to take in, which may distract them from paying attention to your typical rules. Therefore, even if you think your dog is perfectly trained, it is never too late to keep teaching them.

Finding the Root of the Problem

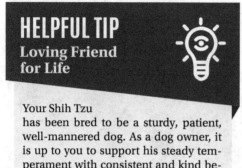

HELPFUL TIP

Loving Friend for Life

Your Shih Tzu has been bred to be a sturdy, patient, well-mannered dog. As a dog owner, it is up to you to support his steady temperament with consistent and kind behavior training. Shih Tzu can be trained as support or therapy dogs, and can even be trained for agility events. Your Shih Tzu will be content around new people and situations if trained and socialized early and often.

When a dog misbehaves, it is not because they want to upset you. Usually, there is a reason behind it that you need to figure out first. These reasons could be different for every dog, but Shih Tzu typically act out when they're jealous or not getting enough attention. They may snap at other dogs if they are worried that you are in danger. They will try to be very protective of you, but even if it sounds like a sweet intention, it can usually be a problem for other dogs and owners. You don't want people to have to avoid your dog just because they snap at other dogs from time to time. You want to make sure you train your dog to behave correctly both at home and in public areas.

If you adopted your dog from a shelter or rescue, the reason behind some of their problems may be because of traumatic events that have happened to them. If they get angry at specific types of dogs, then they may have had bad experiences with them in the past. They also might get scared way too easily at times, which could mean that a previous owner raised them poorly. If your dog acts in any of these ways, then it is important for you to be patient with them and slowly introduce them to these scary concepts. Over time, you can help show them that things aren't the same as they used to be and that you will make sure everything is okay for them. If you suspect that your dog is reacting to some type of trauma that happened in the past, try not to rush them or be too harsh with them or you could end up making them even more scared.

Bad Behavior Prevention

Correcting bad habits and behavior is just like potty training your dog. You can't punish an event that has already occurred. If your dog dug a hole in the yard, you can't yell at them after you find it. You can only scold them when you see them digging it. The same goes for any type of behavior. The second you see your dog doing something they shouldn't

be, firmly tell them no so that they can understand what they did wrong right away.

Once you learn what your dog's bad habits are, slowly ease them into training to help correct them. For example, if you know that your dog barks every time they see another dog, start off by walking them in areas where there are no other dogs and no other distractions around. Then, gradually introduce them to areas with more dogs. This way there will be fewer dogs for them to interact with at first, so if you scold them for barking, it will be easier for them to understand what they did wrong. The sooner they can understand you, the quicker the behavior can be fixed. If you take them to a dog park right away, then there would be too many distractions and too many dogs to bark at, so it would be harder to teach them what they are doing wrong if they start barking. This same method goes for any type of bad behavior such as digging or chewing.

When trying to correct your dog's behavior, remember to avoid punishing them and to reward them when they do things right. The moment you catch them stopping a bad behavior, praise them so they know that not barking is good while barking like crazy is frowned upon. It will take patience just like any other tricks and commands would, so give your dog plenty of time to understand what they should and shouldn't do.

Fixing Bad Habits

"A very unwanted behavior is that Shih Tzu can sometimes show too much interest in their own feces. Picking up their stools quickly can help curb it, and there are some OTC meds, which make stools unpalatable, which will aid in the prevention of this bad habit."

Marion Starr
Starrme Shihtzu

Each dog has different bad habits, but there are many that would be considered common. As mentioned, Shih Tzu are known to bark quite a bit and occasionally dig or chew as many dogs do. However, there are other problems that may not seem like a problem to everyone, but they should still be corrected.

One thing that Shih Tzu will do a lot is chase things. More specifically, their favorite things to chase are small animals such as squirrels, rabbits, and birds. This may not seem like a huge issue since it's cute to watch them try to catch up to a creature that's much faster than they are, but it can become problematic because once your dog spots an animal, it can be hard to control them. If your dog happens to not be on a leash or they pull the leash out of your hand, they could run out of sight or into a busy road if they're not properly trained to stop.

If your dog does pull or chase things often, getting a harness may help to train them better. Having a harness will allow you to take control over your dog easier and will allow you to pull them back better if they try to run off. Walking may not seem like something that needs to be trained, but the better your dog walks with you, the better they will listen to you.

Another bad habit that many dogs share is jumping. When they get excited, Shih Tzu may try to jump up on people to make sure they get as much attention as possible. Since Shih Tzu are small, it may not seem like a big deal to you, but some people may get annoyed if your dog won't stop jumping on them. Take the time to teach them that jumping up on people is not the proper way to get attention.

Shih Tzu are also known to eat things they're not supposed to. This habit is obviously exclusive to Shih Tzu, but many are known to do this. For example, while you are going for a walk, your dog may try to pick up some poop out of the grass or a dead

Photo Courtesy of Sue Cook

worm off the sidewalk when they think you aren't looking. Usually, if you catch them doing it, they will only chew faster and refuse to let go. The best way to teach them out of this bad habit is to keep a close eye on them while walking. If you see them reach for a gross object, pull them away and tell them no as quickly as you can. By repeatedly doing this, they should be able to catch on. You can also keep a treat in your pocket to distract them if you see them heading toward an unwanted substance. Usually, a treat will be much more interesting to them than some random object on the ground.

If your Shih Tzu has a bad habit of eating their own poop while they're outside, then the best solution is to pick it up right away. If you leave their feces scattered throughout your yard for long periods of time, then chances are that they will go out and pick it up eventually. This is why it is important to keep your yard as clean as possible so that your dog does not eat things they are not supposed to.

When to Call a Professional

If you've tried everything you can to fix your dog's behaviors and nothing has changed, then it might be time to call a professional. If you've already gone through basic training courses with your dog, then you should be familiar with seeking help with training, but if not, feel free to ask those you trust for suggestions on trainers. The sooner you contact someone to help you, the sooner the behavior can be corrected. The longer your dog can get away with bad behaviors, the more difficult it will become to correct them, so act fast. A trainer can show you techniques to more effectively train your dog.

CHAPTER 10
Traveling with a Shih Tzu

Photo Courtesy of Michelle Beltran

"Since the Shih Tzu is fairly small and low energy, they generally make good travel companions. The big question is whether you should take them. If you are traveling in a motor home or rent a cottage at the beach, taking your dog along may work very well. You want to make sure your accommodations and activities are going to be dog friendly."

Nancy Lawson
Hill Family Shih Tzu

While your Shih Tzu may seem perfectly content sitting at home, try to travel with them once in a while. This way, if you ever need to travel or move to a new location, your dog will not be shocked at this new experience. It is easy to take your Shih Tzu places due to their small size. Also, because they are hypoallergenic, you don't have to worry about other people's allergies when you take your dog out in public. However, as fun as it is to travel with your dog often, you want to make sure that your dog feels completely comfortable traveling with you at all times, so make sure to ease them into it at first.

Car Rides

Shih Tzu are generally great car companions. They will likely just sleep the whole time or occasionally try to look out the window. However, if you never take them in the car, then this will probably not be the case. Sometimes owners will only take their Shih Tzu in the car if they're going to the vet or the groomer. If you don't regularly take your dog different places, they will associate car rides with those places only, which are generally places that your dog is not a fan of. If this is what they think when they get in the car, then they may pant and tremble every time you drive somewhere with them, which is not a good experience for them.

Bring your Shih Tzu for a car ride every chance you get. This is because the more places you bring your dog, the better travel companion they will be. You need to teach them that car is a good thing, so take them to places that they would enjoy. If they learn that they get to go to

Photo Courtesy of
Annette Henderson

Some dogs do not travel well. They may experience dizziness, vomiting, and nausea. To alleviate these problems, dog owners can take several steps to work toward a solution. Puppies should be allowed to sit in the car with you while it is not in motion. Getting used to the sights and smells of the car will enable your dog to get used to this new environment. When this has been accomplished, short drives will help him become acclimated to the motion and movement of the car.

the park or to a restaurant with outdoor seating when they go in the car, then they will soon get excited when you mention the words "car ride."

For some dogs, even if they enjoy car rides, they will not sit still the whole way there. Since Shih Tzu can be a snuggly breed, they may also try to climb onto your lap while you're driving. While this can be cute, it can also be dangerous if your dog keeps jumping on your lap while you're trying to focus on driving.

One way to help your dog to sit still while driving is to put them in a carrier in the car. This may be a bit scary for your dog at first, but there are lots of different types of carriers made specifically for traveling with your dog. You can try out different ones before deciding which one will be best for your dog. If the carrier is comfortable enough for your Shih Tzu, they may actually prefer traveling in it. Don't expect them to be comfortable in it right away though. They may whine and squirm at first, but after whimpering for a little while, they will likely calm down and fall asleep. Then, after a while they will get used to the carrier and feel comfortable traveling in it.

Another way to keep your dog still in the car is to buy a leash that is designed to buckle to the seatbelt. This way your dog can't freely wander around the car and they will be less of a distraction for you. It is probably best for you to clip the leash to a harness instead of a collar, because if you take a sharp turn, the collar could choke them if the leash is not at an ideal length.

Photo Courtesy of Madison Taylor

Flying with Your Shih Tzu

Many people worry about flying with their dog, but the positive side to bringing a Shih Tzu on a plane is that they are small enough to come in the cabin with you. As long as your dog is under twenty pounds, you can keep them in an airplane carrier under your seat during the flight. This way, you know your dog is right next to you at all times and you do not need to worry about them while you're in the air. There is usually an extra fee of at least seventy-five dollars to bring a pet with you, but it varies between different airlines. Make sure to research the different airline pet policies ahead of time to find out which one is right for you.

HELPFUL TIP
Travel Smart

People are on the move and often choose to take their pets with them. Whether you are planning to take short trips in the car or will transport your pet via air, do your homework to ensure the safety and comfort of your pet. To travel in cars with their dogs, some dog owners purchase pet car seats that hold the dog safely and comfortably in the back seat of the car. Dogs should not be allowed to roam inside the car; this is dangerous to the pet and hazardous to people. A small dog can get caught around the driver's feet, a very serious situation.

Before flying with your dog for the first time, make sure to visit your vet. They can help you decide if you should give your dog any medication during the flight. If your Shih Tzu is generally calm and laid back, then they will probably just sleep through the flight with no problem. However, if your Shih Tzu is typically full of energy, then you will likely need to give them something to calm them down. No one wants to sit by a dog that's squirming and barking throughout the whole flight.

You can find an airplane carrier online, but the best way to go about it is to go into the pet store with your dog so you can try different ones out. Some of them can be kind of pricey, but you want to make sure you find one that your dog is comfortable in. Some can be held over your shoulder while others have wheels so you can pull your dog behind you without having to carry them the whole time. Your dog is supposed to stay in the carrier in the airport and throughout the entire flight, so don't just select the cheapest option if your dog won't be comfortable in it.

Technically, your dog must remain under your seat the whole time with the carrier closed, but many airlines are lenient about this. It can be scary for your dog to stay in the carrier the whole flight, so usually it is okay for you to let their head stick out during the flight so they can at least see that you're right there beside them. Even if you plan to

HELPFUL TIP
Avoid Travel Issues

Some owners choose to crate their dogs while in the car as well. Practice small trips with your pet and graduate to longer ones. If your dog tends to get carsick, feed him dry biscuits or snacks prior to traveling. While traveling longer distances, schedule a break every 30 minutes along the way until your dog is acclimated to car travel. If nausea remains and is a chronic problem, or if your dog does not settle once on the road, don't hesitate to consult your veterinarian. There are organic, calming treatments that your vet can offer to make travel easier for you and your pet.

let your Shih Tzu look around on the flight, you should still be prepared to close the carrier if a flight attendant requests that you do.

Before taking your dog to the airport, make sure to use the bag ahead of time. Try putting them in it at home and giving them a treat if they sit still or allow you to close the bag. Practice carrying them around in it so that they can get used to the feeling of being in their airplane carrier. The more time they spend in the carrier ahead of time, the more relaxed they will be when they sit in it on the plane ride.

Make sure to take your dog outside as close to your flight as possible. There is nowhere for your dog to pee on the plane besides in their carrier, so you want to make sure they go ahead of time. Some airports have specific dog relief areas where you can take your dog to the bathroom in the airport. Don't rely on this though because sometimes they are indoor areas with fake grass, so your dog may not see this as an okay place to do their business. Even if your dog has gone out right before your flight, make sure to bring some paper towels on the plane with you just in case your dog happens to have an accident.

Bringing your dog through airport security for the first time can be a bit intimidating because they don't give much information about that process ahead of time. If you're in a busy airport, it actually makes going through security quicker, because they will usually allow you to go through the handicap line if they see that you have your dog with you. Then, once you get to the front of the line, you will want to take your dog out of the airplane bag. You will send the bag through the machine with your other belongings, but you will carry your Shih Tzu through the metal detector. Security will help you if you have any questions, but usually after going through the metal detector, they will ask to test your hands quick. Once you have gone through this process once, it should become much easier for you the next time you fly with your dog.

Staying in a Hotel

Not all hotels are dog-friendly, so do plenty of research if you are planning to stay overnight somewhere with your dog. Many hotels will allow dogs in certain rooms as long as you pay a small fee. Every hotel charges different amounts and has different requirements about what dogs are allowed. Luckily, since Shih Tzu are a small, easygoing breed, it is easier to find hotels that will accept them.

A hotel will be a strange place for your pup, so remember to bring plenty of items along that will smell like home to them. If you have to leave your Shih Tzu alone in the hotel room often, make sure they have plenty of accessible places to sleep and lots of their toys scattered about. You can even push a chair up against the window if it is too high for your dog to see out of. This way, your dog will feel more at home and get less scared if you leave.

Since the hotel allows dogs, then it is likely that your dog is not the only visitor. If your Shih Tzu can smell other dogs or hear them barking from other rooms, they may feel compelled to bark as well. Try your best to train them to avoid this behavior, but they may not listen as well in this unfamiliar area. All the rooms with dogs in them are usually kept close to each other, so expect the occasional barking conversation between dogs in other rooms.

Similar to their first night home at your place, the first night in a hotel may be restless for them. Many people will be coming and going at all hours of the day and night, so your dog may wake up every time they hear noises outside. Instead of yelling at them to go back to sleep, pet them and give them attention so they understand that everything is okay.

Kennels

Kenneling dogs is a common solution when you're going to be out of town, but if you decide to do this with your Shih Tzu, then there are lots of things to consider. Not all kennels are the same, so do research ahead of time to find a trustworthy one for your dog.

One positive of keeping your dog at a kennel is that they are constantly monitored by professionals. Some kennels will even have a way for you to watch your dog online to make sure everything is going well. However, if a kennel does not seem trustworthy, then they may not provide your dog with this same safety, so be careful. Look for a kennel with a good reputation. Find one that cares about your dog and not just the

Photo Courtesy of Mollie Doucette

money. You can get good recommendations from vets, groomers, and local pet stores.

Some kennels may not provide your dog with the amount of exercise and attention that they need, especially if they have a lot of different dogs to look after. They may try to charge you extra for extra playtime. These are the types of kennels that you want to avoid. You shouldn't have to pay extra for your dog to get what they usually get at home. You also will want to find a kennel that will allow you to bring your own food for the dog. If the kennel provides their own food, it may not be the best brand for your dog and they may get sick from the sudden change in diet.

Your dog is always most comfortable in a familiar environment. A kennel can be new and scary to them, which is why many people will avoid taking their dogs there. You may want to take your dog to the kennel first to check it out, just so they aren't surprised when they are suddenly dropped off and you're no longer with them.

One last thing to be mindful of when taking your dog to a kennel is to make sure your dog is up to date on all possible vaccinations. There are diseases that can be spread at kennels, such kennel cough. You want to ensure your dog is not harmed while they are staying there.

Dog Sitters

A pet sitter can be a better option when leaving your dog alone, but only if it is someone that you trust. There are professionals that you can hire to watch your dog, but you can also just choose a close friend or family member to watch your Shih Tzu while you are away. Whoever you choose, make sure it is someone your dog can meet ahead of time so that you are not just leaving them with a stranger.

When allowing someone to watch your pet, you can either have them stop by your house to check on your dog frequently or you can have your dog stay with them. There are pros and cons to each option, so it is important to decide which one would work better for you and your dog.

If you choose to allow the pet sitter into your home while you're out of town, make sure that it is not only someone you trust with your dog, but also with everything in your house. If the pet sitter comes to your house, then your dog does not have to go to an unfamiliar setting. Everything will smell like you and it can help them feel more comfortable being left alone for a while. Your pet sitter can also pick up your mail and packages while they're there if that would benefit you as well.

*Photo Courtesy of
Mallory Duffy*

Keeping your dog at home could be an issue though, because then they won't have someone with them at all times. If your Shih Tzu does not stay in their crate, they may not have a problem roaming around by themselves, but sometimes they prefer the extra company, rather than having someone just stop by to feed them and take them out.

If you allow your dog to stay at someone else's house, make sure it is a place that your dog has visited beforehand. You want to make sure they've had plenty of time to smell and explore the area before they actually have to stay there. This can be a better idea if you don't want to give your sitter a key to your house.

Make sure to bring everything your dog might need to the dog sitter's house. Give them enough food for the whole time, bring plenty of their toys, and take a blanket or pillow of your own so they can have something that smells like you. The more stuff you bring with them, the more at home they will feel while you're gone.

CHAPTER 11
Nutrition

What you feed your dog plays a huge role in their overall health. Don't just pick the cheapest food brand or feed them only when it's convenient for you. Because you want to make sure your pup is well fed and given everything they need to grow up strong and healthy, put careful consideration into what you feed your dog on a day-to-day basis.

Importance of a Good Diet

HELPFUL TIP
Table Scraps

Most dog owners enjoy sharing small scraps with their four-legged friends. We may believe we are being kind by offering "people treats" to dogs, but in fact, we may be harming them. Be aware of the human foods that should never be given to dogs by checking the list offered by the American Kennel Club (akc.org).

There a lot of different dog food brands and flavors to choose from, so put a lot of thought into which one to give your dog. Dogs need a good mix of nutrients just like people do. The food you select for your dog can greatly affect how happy and healthy they become over time.

When you bring your Shih Tzu home, there was likely a certain brand that they were being fed ahead of time. Their breeder or foster parents can inform you about this specific food brand. Keep feeding them that brand at first until you can find something better for them. When switching brands of food, start off by gradually mixing the two together to avoid upsetting your dog's stomach.

Dogs can be allergic to different ingredients in dog foods that many owners wouldn't expect. A big one is grain. If your dog is suddenly getting sick often, it could be because there's grain in their food. Luckily, there are lots of grain-free dog food brands and dog treats to choose from to help avoid upsetting your dog's stomach.

Another ingredient that can upset a dog's stomach that many owners don't even consider is chicken. Chicken is a common flavor that most dogs love, but it can make some dogs sick if they eat too much of it. If your dog is getting sick and you are unsure of the reason, you may want to try switching to a food that doesn't have grain or chicken.

Recommended Food for a Shih Tzu

"We always recommend high quality food for our adults and puppies. Some Shih Tzu can have food allergies. The most common ones are Chicken and Corn. If your Shih Tzu is having itchy skin, frequent ear infections, or any other allergy symptoms try eliminating these two to see if the symptoms improve."

Monica Cox
Maple Lane Pups

Since Shih Tzu are a smaller breed, make sure the food you give them comes in pieces that are small enough for them to chew. Some brands of food make food specifically for smaller dogs. If your Shih Tzu has no interest in chewing dry foods, you can explore canned dog food or a raw food diet. You can ask your local pet store for suggestions on the best options for your dog. However, while wet dog food can typically be more interesting to your dog, it can sometimes make their breath and their poop smell a bit worse, so be especially careful with which flavor you select.

Photo Courtesy of Kay Alexander

When deciding on a dog food brand, look for brands that are high in protein. These foods will be more expensive, but will typically be much healthier for your dog. On the bag, it should say the percentage of protein that is used in the food.

Karen DeAngelo, a Shih Tzu breeder from Glory Ridge Shih Tzu, explains that Shih Tzu "cannot tolerate soy. Food can cause bladder stones and bile vomiting." Therefore, when selecting a food for your dog, check the ingredients to ensure that there is no soy included. It may not be bad for every single Shih Tzu, but it is a common ingredient for this breed to get sick from.

When looking for dog food, you can either choose from a small, local pet store or a big chain. Chains are popular because they carry a large variety of food brands to choose from and are easily accessible. Local stores carry a smaller selection of foods, but they typically carry only healthier brands that sometimes cannot be bought at just any store. They also can give you more personal advice on what to purchase for your dog.

If your dog is picky, you can switch up the flavors of the food once in a while to keep them interested. However, try to keep the same brand if possible so your dog will not get sick from the sudden change. If your dog is picky no matter what, you can purchase different food toppers to mix with the food to make it more appealing for your dog.

Finding Treats

People don't always think about treats as carefully as they do about food, but they can also affect your dog's health.

Shih Tzu typically prefer smaller, softer treats because they're easier for them to chew. The flavor varies from dog to dog, but chicken, bacon, cheese, and pumpkin are typically favorites for most dogs. Some small pet stores will allow you to mix and match different treats to help your dog choose which flavor they like best.

Even though they are small, Shih Tzu enjoy chewing on different types of bones and chews such as bully sticks or pig ears. These can help keep them occupied because they're like a treat and a toy all in one. When selecting a chew for your dog, make sure to use something healthy. Avoid anything with rawhide in it because it can be difficult for your dog to digest completely.

HELPFUL TIP
Quality is Key

Your Shih Tzu is a sturdy little dog. However, he needs quality food to maintain his health and wellness. Consulting your vet or breeder regarding which nutritious food to offer your dog is the pathway to lifelong wellness. Whether you purchase dog food or prepare your own homemade pet food, consult professionals to ensure your pet is getting the nutrition he needs. Care should be taken to offer age-appropriate food at the various stages of your dog's life. Puppy, adult, senior, and weight-control foods are widely available. Your Shih Tzu may tend to gain weight, so be mindful of the appropriate amount of food he needs daily.

People Foods to Avoid

No almonds should be given to dogs because they may block the esophagus or tear the dog's windpipe. Other nuts that are considered toxic are pecans, walnuts, and macadamia nuts. Cashews can be given to dogs according to the AKC, however, in moderation and only unsalted varieties.

Humans love chocolate, but it is dangerous for dogs to consume. Chocolate may cause diarrhea, vomiting, and even seizures.

Cinnamon is not toxic but can cause mouth irritation in dogs. It is best avoided. The AKC says no to garlic and onions because of their toxicity, and owners should not offer ice cream to their dogs. Be cautious when giving any dairy products, including yogurt, to dogs, as they may be lactose intolerant.

Whenever you're eating at your dining room table, it is likely that you will look down and see your little Shih Tzu staring back up at you with puppy dog eyes. Don't be tempted to give in. As tasty as human food can be to your pup, much of it can be extremely unhealthy and even toxic to your dog. The occasional crumb seems like it can't hurt, but it's important to know which people foods to completely avoid.

Almost everyone is familiar with the fact that chocolate is like a poison to dogs. Not only chocolate, but also coffee and anything else with caffeine in it. If your dog gets a hold of some chocolate, they may not immediately get sick, but the smaller the dog is, the less they need to consume to be harmed by it. Also, the darker the chocolate, the worse it is for your dog. Therefore, it is important that you keep all types of chocolate and caffeine far out of reach from your pup.

Another dangerous food for your dog to consume is grapes or raisins. While most other fruits and vegetables are good for dogs, grapes can cause kidney failure to your pet. It is unknown exactly why these little fruits are so toxic, but it is important to keep them away from your dog as well.

Avoid giving dairy to your dog. Too much dairy can upset their stomachs and give them diarrhea. As much as they love milk, cheese, and ice cream, too much can become very unhealthy for your dog. Luckily, they are human foods that you can easily find healthier substitutes for. Many pet stores sell goat milk and dog ice cream, which can be much better for your dog and they will enjoy it just as much.

Another human food that many people don't realize is bad for your dog is bones. After eating a chicken leg, sometimes people think they can let their dog chew on the bone, but this should never be the case. Unlike bones you can purchase at the pet store, chicken bones can easily splinter and choke your dog. Do not allow your dog to chew on something unless you know it is perfectly safe for them. Also, do not give your dog the fat trimmings of your meat. Whether that fat is cooked or uncooked, it has been known to cause pancreatitis.

Along with bones and fat trimmings, raw meat is another food that should be avoided. Just like for humans, any type of raw meat, fish, or eggs that your dog ingests can have bacteria on it and cause food poisoning. If your dog accidentally gets a hold of any of these substances, it will likely cause vomiting and you will want to get your dog checked out by a vet.

It may seem harmless to slip your dog the occasional French fry or potato chip, but these salty foods should really only be given to your pet in very small portions if at all. Salt can be a lot for your dog to handle and if given in large portions can cause them to vomit or get diarrhea. However, if the food has garlic or onions on it, then that is toxic for your dog and should be avoided just as chocolate or grapes would.

Humans Foods that Are Safe

While there are lots of human foods to steer clear of, there are some that are okay to feed your dog once in a while. However, you should not make it a habit. If you are unsure whether or not a type of food is safe for your dog to eat, research it first before giving it to your dog.

Most meats are okay for your dog to eat as long as they are cooked properly. Salmon is one of the best sources of protein for dogs and can help with

HELPFUL TIP
Safe Foods

On the AKC-approved list of human foods for dogs are turkey, chicken, pork, rice, corn, and quinoa. Honey, in very small amounts, may be given to dogs. Honey contains vitamins A, B, C, D, E, and K along with potassium, magnesium, copper, and antioxidants. Moderation is key when offering human foods to dogs.

your dog's joints and give their immune system a boost as well. Other

meats, such as turkey and ham, are also okay for your dog to consume as long as there is no garlic, salt, or other seasoning included in it. Also, make sure that there are no bones in the meat that your dog could accidentally choke on. As long as the meat is cooked to ensure that there are no parasites on it, then it is safe for your dog to eat.

Another common human food that dogs can safely eat is peanut butter. It is a favorite flavor among dogs and is often included in different types of treats and bones at the pet store. It can be an excellent source of protein for your dog and spreading a little on their dog food can help them to eat more often if they are typically picky with their food.

A lot of fruits and vegetables are also safe for your dog to eat, but make sure you know ahead of time which ones are safest for your dog. Apples, oranges, bananas, watermelon, strawberries, and blueberries are all examples of fruits that are both healthy and tasty for your dog. However, try to take out any seeds, stems, and leaves because these can cause problems if they eat too much of them.

As for vegetables, carrots, green beans, peas, and broccoli are examples of safe foods for your dog. Not all dogs are a fan of vegetables since they don't have much of a taste compared to other human foods, but if your dog enjoys vegetables, then they can become a healthy alternative to their typical dog treats. As with any other human foods, try not to give veggies to them too often or they could upset your dog's stomach.

One human food that is often a favorite for dogs is cheese. As soon as they hear you open a bag of shredded cheese or rip the wrapping of string cheese, your Shih Tzu will typically appear right beside you with wide eyes. While cheese is not necessarily bad for your dog, it is a type of dairy, so it should only be given to your dog in moderation. If your dog gets sick from cheese, it is possible that they are lactose intolerant, so you may want to consult your vet about it.

While these foods are safe for your dogs to consume, make sure not to give too much to your dog at once. They may beg, but sometimes it is okay to just say no to your dog. They can't expect that every time they beg they are going to get table scraps.

Weight Management

If you notice that your Shih Tzu is beginning to get a little chunky, then you need to start paying closer attention to everything they're eating. A little extra exercise can always help out, but a lot of times, people are feeding their dogs too much without even realizing it.

When feeding your dog their meals each day, make sure to carefully measure out the amount. Don't just grab a handful or guess how much to put in the bowl. The back of the food bag you purchase should tell you exactly how much to serve for your dog's weight. Keep that size measuring cup right by the dog food at all times. This way you know you won't forget to give your dog the correct amount of food.

If you have been regularly feeding your dog just like you are supposed to and they're still gaining weight, then you may want to cut back on their serving sizes. They likely won't even notice if you give them a slightly smaller amount at each meal. By doing this, you can help them to get their weight back on track.

A dog's weight also has a lot to do with the treats you give them. It can be hard to resist giving your dog a little something every time they give you a longing gaze, but this is a habit that you need to learn to break. Treats may not have a ton of calories in each little bite, but if you are giving them rewards too often, then those calories can easily add up. If you want to praise your dog, play with them and pet them more often to substitute for the smaller amounts of treats. If you are giving your pup the attention they deserve, then they likely won't even notice that they're getting fewer snacks.

CHAPTER 12
Grooming Your Shih Tzu

"They usually need to be taken to a groomer every 4 to 6 weeks. I recommend that people do some minor grooming at home, especially around their faces. This makes it easier on the groomers and also it's nicer for the dogs if you learn to keep their faces and eyes cleaned up at home."

Lisa McKinney
Mr. Foo's Shih Tzu

Regardless of the length of your Shih Tzu's hair, they need to be groomed often. Take the time to find a groomer that you trust, and they can help you maintain your Shih Tzu's health grooming wise. There are lots of different haircuts and services that you can choose from for your dog, so consider your options carefully.

Photo Courtesy of Lisa McKinney

Coat Basics

The reason some dogs need frequent grooming while others do not is because dogs that don't shed have hair instead of fur. If a dog has fur, their coat naturally sheds on its own and does not need a groomer to cut it. If a dog has hair like a Shih Tzu does, then it will just keep growing like a human's hair would until you get it cut. This is why Shih Tzu need to visit the groomer regularly to maintain a soft coat.

Not everyone prefers the same haircut for their dog. Some owners like to keep their Shih Tzu's hair long and flowing while others like to keep them shaved. When you visit the groomer, you can give them suggestions as to what you specifically want. Typically, if you live in a warmer climate or if you take your dog outside a lot, you may want to keep a shorter haircut to avoid them getting hot or dirty.

No matter the length you choose for your Shih Tzu's hair, try to get them into the groomer every four to six weeks. If you find a groomer that you like, you can make regular appointments to make sure your pup stays clean and well groomed.

Bathing and Brushing

"If they are groomed consistently and brushed in between, they will shed very little."

Debbie Heuston
Debbie's Darlings

Photo Courtesy of Heather Reid

Your Shih Tzu ideally should be brushed at least once a week. The longer their hair is, the more often you should brush them to avoid their hair getting matted. If you take your dog to the groomer when they have mats in them, then the groomer will try their best to brush those mats out, but if they're too bad, they may need to shave your dog. If this happens, don't get upset at the groomer, because your dog's hair will grow back in no time. If their hair seems to get matted easily, you will want to start brushing them more often.

It is a good idea to bathe your Shih Tzu about every three weeks, or whenever they get excessively dirty. For example, if they dig a hole at the dog park, you should probably bathe them as soon as possible to get all the dirt out of their hair. When you get your dog groomed, they will also get a bath with the full groom, so unless you cut their hair yourself, you do not need to bathe them on your own very often.

When your Shih Tzu is still a puppy, you will want to bathe them a little more frequently. Puppies have a bad habit of getting into things they're not supposed to and can get dirty much easier. Also, when puppies are getting housetrained, they can sometimes get feces stuck to them when they go to the bathroom, so make sure you wash that off to avoid infections.

Nail Trimming

Try to get your Shih Tzu's nails trimmed at least once a month. This is also included with a full groom, but if you only rely on them getting trimmed when they get their haircut, then their nails may get a bit long. If your dog's nails make a loud clicking sound when they walk, this means they probably should be trimmed.

Most groomers will allow walk-ins to stop by for a quick nail trim. Usually about once a month is good, but if you haven't trimmed them in a while, then the blood vessels in your dog's nails, which are referred to as quicks, could have grown too long. If their quicks are long, then the groomer will not be able to cut their nail completely to avoid cutting the quick and causing bleeding. To get your dog's quicks back to a healthy length, the groomer will likely tell you to come in every other week until their nails start growing normally again. This may seem like a lot of work, but this way your dog's nails will be more comfortable for them and they won't scratch you if they jump up on your legs.

If you don't want to pay to get your dog's nails trimmed every time, then you can trim them yourself. You can buy your own nail clippers for dogs and trim their nails whenever they get long. However, make sure you research the length that their nails are supposed to be, so you can avoid cutting them too short. If you accidentally trim their nails too short, that can traumatize your dog and make them not want you touching their feet ever again. It won't take long for the nail to heal if you do this, but of course, it doesn't feel good to know that you hurt your dog. If they do bleed a lot, you can use cornstarch to stop the bleeding. You can also gently dip it in flour or baking soda until the bleeding stops.

When cutting your dog's nails, don't forget to trim the dewclaws as well. These are the nails on your dog's feet that typically rest higher up than the other nails. They are often forgotten about because not all dogs have them. However, they grow just as fast as normal nails do, which means if they are forgotten, they can start growing into your dog's foot, which can be extremely uncomfortable for them. Make sure to maintain your dog's nails to avoid them growing at unhealthy lengths.

Some Shih Tzu just dislike their feet being touched no matter what, so it may be difficult to get them to sit still. You may want to have someone help hold your dog while you're trimming their nails so you don't make any mistakes. Always reward your dog when they are good for a nail trim. This will help make the process less scary for them knowing that there's a reward at the end.

Photo Courtesy of
Dr. Troy Clifford Dargin

Brushing Teeth

Teeth brushing is one area of dog grooming that many owners neglect. A Shih Tzu can easily get gum disease when they are older, so it is important to keep their teeth as clean as possible as they grow up.

The easiest way to keep up with their teeth is to buy a toothbrush and toothpaste for dogs and brush them at least once a week. However, the more often you brush their teeth, the better off they will be. Wait until your dog calms down to try brushing their teeth so that they are less likely to freak out and squirm away. You should reward them after they cooperate, so that they can get used to this process.

Try to find a toothpaste that tastes good to your pet. If they like the flavor, then they will be less likely to fear getting their teeth brushed. They still will probably dislike the feeling of the toothbrush against their teeth, but at least they should be more tolerant of it.

If your dog hates their teeth being brushed no matter what you do, then there are other options too. There are lots of toys and chews that clean your dog's teeth while they chew on them, but some definitely work better than others. Ask around and find out which brands are recommended and which ones will have the greatest effect on your dog's teeth.

It is easy to forget about teeth cleaning from time to time. If it's been a while, you may notice your dog's breath starting to smell more than usual and their teeth may not look as presentable anymore. If this is the case, then you can get a deep cleaning done on their teeth. This can be done at the vet or sometimes small pet stores will host special teeth cleaning days. Usually, your dog will need to be put under at the vet for this procedure, but if your dog is better behaved, then there are some non-anesthetic options that you can try. However, if your dog refuses to cooperate, then they may not be able to do the non-anesthetic procedure. Your Shih Tzu's health is in their best interest and they would not want to hurt your dog while cleaning their teeth.

Photo Courtesy of
Michelle Beltran

Cleaning Ears and Eyes

If you are looking for a low-maintenance dog, a Shih Tzu may not be for you. This lovely dog has a double coat that needs daily brushing. Be prepared to bathe your dog every three to four weeks to keep his coat smooth and silky. Some owners use a spray-on conditioner between regular baths to allow for easy brushing. Gently clean your Shih Tzu's eyes with a soft, clean damp cloth daily. Do this carefully and often. Nail trimming is also important and a task you may want to leave to professionals. Do not be put off by the high maintenance requirements for the Shih Tzu, however. Many owners choose to have their dog groomed and trimmed in a "puppy cut."

Eyes and ears are areas that will also be cleaned during a haircut, but with Shih Tzu, their ears and eyes sometimes need extra attention.

If you notice your Shih Tzu scratching their ears often, this could be a sign that they need to be cleaned more. You can buy ear drops to help clean out their ears, but they will not like the feeling of a liquid going down their ears at first. Give them a treat if you clean their ears this way. If they still continue to scratch, you may want to consult a groomer or vet to make sure they don't have an infection.

Shih Tzu get tear stains fairly frequently, so cleaning their eyes is a must. If you notice that it is crusty or slimy under their eyes, make sure to wipe it off as soon as possible. You want to make sure their eyes are always clear of any dirt or grime. If your Shih Tzu tries to eat the crust that you pick off their eyes, do not let them. Give them a treat instead because it is not healthy for them to eat their eye goop. It could easily upset their stomach and make them sick.

If your Shih Tzu is white around their face, then their tears will stain the fur with a strange brown color. There are products that can be used to help fix this and your groomer can suggest the best way to keep their face clean and free of any gross substances.

Sheila Spink of Emerald City Shih Tzu suggests that owners should "keep the hair from their eyes as they can develop eye ulcers if they get scratched by the hair." This is why Shih Tzu with longer hair are so often seen with bows and clips pulling the hair on their heads away from their eyes. Not only can the hair around their face make it harder for them to see, but it can also get stuck in their eye and scratch it, causing even more eye issues for your Shih Tzu. The more you keep your Shih Tzu's eyes clear of unwanted substances, the better off they will be.

Going to the Groomer

While it may be cheaper to always cut your dog's hair yourself, many people find it easier and more efficient to let a groomer do it. The groom will include all of the other grooming basics, which can help take some extra work off your shoulders. Before you let your puppy get their first groom, you will want to make sure that they have all of their required vaccinations.

When looking for a groomer for your dog, it is important to settle on someone that you trust. They should clearly care about your dog and should want to work with you as much as possible in order to give your dog the perfect haircut for you. Typically, groomers at larger pet stores are not the best option for your pup because they are much larger and busier than they would be at a vet or local pet store. If you get your dog groomed at a large pet store, then there may be too many distractions, which could easily freak your Shih Tzu out. It also could be difficult for you to form a relationship with the groomer since they have such a large number of clients coming and going. Therefore, it is better to find a groomer at a smaller shop so that your dog can feel less stressed when going to get their haircut.

Some groomers specialize in certain breeds, so if you can find a groomer that knows a lot about different haircuts for Shih Tzu, then this may be your best bet. Even if you don't want anything fancy done to your dog's hair, it can be beneficial to give your dog to a groomer who knows a lot about the specific breed because they are likely better at controlling this breed and keeping them calm during the haircut. Different breeds can act in different ways, so finding someone who works with the Shih Tzu breed often can help put you at ease knowing that you're leaving your dog with a groomer you trust.

You can research the different groom-

*Photo Courtesy of
Cathy Panuelos*

ers in the area and read reviews about them ahead of time. Sometimes the closest one will not necessarily be the best fit for you. Some will also be cheaper than others, but remember that cheaper haircuts will probably not be better, although that's not always the case.

It is good to get to know your groomer as a person too, so they can be closer to your dog. As your groomer gets to know you and your dog better, they can give you tips on different products to maintain your dog's health and needs.

Many dogs are scared of getting groomed, but the more often they do it, the more likely they are to become used to the process. However, if your dog seems completely terrified every time they come and go from the groomer then this could be a sign that your dog is not being treated well there. You don't really get to see what goes on in the grooming room while you are not there, so if your dog is petrified of going to one groomer and more at ease when they go to another, this can definitely help you to decide which one is a better match for you and your dog. Your Shih Tzu can be very smart when it comes to which people they trust, so listen to them if it seems like they are trying to warn you about something, especially when it comes to something serious like grooming. Shih Tzu breeder Twila Severance from Divine Design Shih Tzu explains that "any signs of fear with a groomer is a sign to find a new one. The dog is telling you something, and you should listen." You don't want just anyone using scissors so close to your pup.

When Professional Help Is Necessary

Going to the groomer doesn't just have to be for a full haircut. If your dog will not cooperate when you try to trim their nails or brush their teeth, then it may be time to ask a professional such as a groomer or vet to help. They are used to dealing with difficult dogs, so they should have no problem caring for your dog's needs.

A professional can also help give you tips as to what might make it easier for you to maintain your dog's health yourself. Many people just prefer to go to groomers for these small services because it saves time and the results are usually better.

If bathing your dog is a pain, the groomer can also bathe your dog as well. This will typically include the nails and ears, so you don't need to come in for separate appointments to get all those things done. You don't have to find a professional to groom and take care of your dog's health, but sometimes it can help a lot.

CHAPTER 13
Basic Health Care

Taking care of your new dog is much more than just training and giving attention. Making sure your Shih Tzu stays in perfect health is also an important part of having a dog. Don't neglect visiting a vet often or giving your dog all necessary medications; doing so could greatly hurt your dog, so always try your best to stay on top of it.

Visiting the Vet

Even if your dog seems perfectly healthy to you, this doesn't mean that you should avoid visiting the vet. A yearly checkup is usually ideal for your dog to make sure that they are up to date on all the vaccinations they may need. Your vet can also answer any questions or concerns you may have. Even if something seems minor to you, it can't hurt to ask about it during your checkup to ensure that your dog is healthy.

Always have your vet's number saved in your phone or written down in a place that is easily accessible to you. This way if you ever have an emergency with your dog or need to ask a question as soon as possible, you can get in immediate contact with your local vet. You never want to wait until the last minute when it comes to anything related to your dog's health.

Vaccinations

When visiting your vet, they will tell you about all the vaccinations that are recommended for your dog. If you are unsure about what a specific vaccination prevents, your vet can give you all of the details about it before you decide to give the dog the vaccination. It is okay to opt out on certain vaccinations, but usually those who are knowledgeable about dogs, such as breeders or groomers, can help to suggest which vaccinations are absolutely necessary and which ones should be avoided. There may be certain ones that are not good for Shih Tzu to get, so it is important to do your research ahead of time.

Photo Courtesy of Madison Taylor

While many shots are recommended, there are some that are required, especially if you are going to take your dog on a plane or board them. Nobody wants to risk their dog getting sick, so if you are leaving your dog somewhere with a lot of other dogs, you will want to make sure they are up to date on all the required vaccinations. Vaccinations are beneficial because the more dogs that are immune to certain diseases, the fewer dogs that can spread the disease.

When your dog gets a shot, the vet will give you paperwork to prove which vaccines they have received. Hold onto this since you don't always know when you might need it. Some airlines, kennels, and groomers may require you to show them proof that your pup is vaccinated, so make sure you have easy access to these records just in case.

If you get a puppy, it is important to keep them away from other animals until they have had all their required vaccinations. You don't want to risk your dog catching any diseases while they are out and you don't want to put any other animals in danger. Once your puppy has all of their shots, then they are free to go out in public as much as you want them to.

Fleas and Ticks

If your dog spends a lot of time outside, then bugs are definitely something you should be concerned about. Shih Tzu usually have thick, dark-colored fur, so if a flea or tick climbs onto your dog, it will be hard for you to notice it right away. Check them regularly for fleas and ticks, especially if they appear to be scratching more often than usual. In warmer climates, these pests are more common because they can be out year-round, making them more dangerous for your dog.

There are lots of options for flea and tick prevention. They will almost always keep away both pests, so you don't need to worry about buying two different preventions. Some brands can simply be bought at the store, but these options are not as strong as something a vet would provide. This is because the store-bought flea medicine is usually applied to your dog's back while the vet will usually give you one that your dog can actually ingest. The first option is not bad, it is a good option to

Photo Courtesy of
Natalie Piccolo

start off with, but if it doesn't seem to be keeping the bugs away, then you need to consult your vet to get a prescription for a stronger flea and tick medicine.

If you live in an area that snows during the winter, then you don't need to give your dog the medicine when it's too cold for the bugs to be out. However, if it's warm year-round near you, then you always have to give your dog the medicine. Most types will be needed once a month, but there are some that you only need to give them every three months. It all depends on which one works best for your dog.

If you catch a flea or tick on your dog, try your best not to freak out. If your dog can sense that you're worried, then they will worry too, which will make them less cooperative when you try to get the flea or tick off of them.

With pulling out a tick, you must be extremely careful. Shih Tzu already don't like it when people pick at their fur, but they especially will not be a fan if you are pulling up a bug that is biting onto them. Make sure you hold on as close to the dog's skin as possible when you pull to make sure that the head does not break off from the body. If the tick appears to have been clinging to your dog for a while, then you may want to visit a vet afterward to make sure that your dog did not get Lyme disease from the tick.

If you spot a flea on your dog, grab it immediately and kill it to make sure it doesn't lay eggs in your dog's fur. Fleas can be tricky to kill; they won't just squish between your fingers. You can usually break them in half with your fingernails; if you drop dish soap on them, they will usually die instantly. You have to be very careful with fleas because they are tiny and can jump farther than you'd expect, so if you lose a flea in your house while trying to get it off your dog, then your best option would be to clean everything in that area to ensure that it did not survive.

Once you find one flea, it does not automatically mean that your house is infested with them. Your dog could have easily just picked one up outside, but just to be safe, you should give your dog a bath with flea shampoo as soon as you can. This will kill all of the fleas that are currently on your dog, but the flea bath itself will not stop your dog from picking up more pests. This is why it is important to get use some type of flea and tick prevention ahead of time.

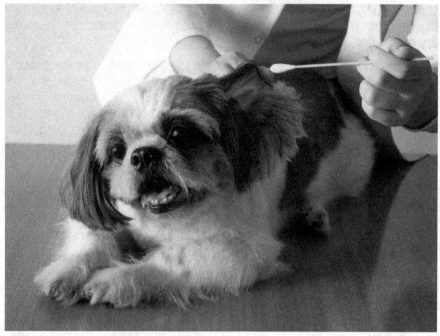

Worms and Parasites

Ticks and fleas may seem the most concerning because they are bugs that you can actually see on your dog, but there are also worms and parasites that you need to worry about preventing as well. The most common one is heartworm. If your dog needs to get treated for heartworm, then they are not supposed to exercise or run around much for six months after. For Shih Tzu, this is not always a problem, but if your dog has a lot of energy, then it can be a difficult thing to deal with.

You can get heartworm medication from your vet. It is usually a chewable substance that actually tastes good to your dog. They won't even realize that it is medicine. You need to give it to your pet once a month year-round despite the weather to completely protect them from it.

The most common way for your dog to get worms and parasites inside them is for your dog to accidentally ingest parasite eggs. This can happen when your dog tries to eat contaminated soil, water, or grass outside. Shih Tzu love to stick their nose in places that they shouldn't when they are outside, so it is important to stop your dog from eating different substances outside. If they eat too much grass or lick up a dirty puddle, they could accidentally lick up some unwanted substances and parasites along with it, allowing them to get sick. Make sure to keep a close eye on your dog outside to ensure that they do not ingest anything unhealthy.

Common Diseases and Conditions

"The biggest issue with Shih Tzu can be associated with the short nose. Most Shih Tzu do snort some. It does seem though to be much more prominent during the time they are teething. In and of itself, snorting is not a major deal as long as there is not green or milky discharge from the nose."

Nancy Lawson
Hill Family Shih Tzu

Not all dogs will have the same problems as they grow up, but there are some common conditions among Shih Tzu. If you get your dog from a breeder, they should be able to notify you of any genetic health concerns. However, if you adopted a rescue, it is difficult to know their backgrounds and genetic history, so it may be hard to guess what types of conditions they could get over time.

One health concern that is common for Shih Tzu is that as they grow older, due to their large eyes, they can get a lot of eye issues, such as infections and loss of eyesight. If a Shih Tzu's eyes are not cleaned often, then materials can easily get stuck in their eyes due to their shallow eye sockets. The best way to ensure that a Shih Tzu's eyes stay as clean as possible is to check them every day to make sure there is no redness or discoloration. If their eyes water a lot or appear cloudy, then this may be something that you want to check out with your vet. The longer you wait to get their eyes checked out, the worse it will be in the end. Eye problems almost always need immediate attention when it comes to the Shih Tzu breed.

Ears are also another problem spot for Shih Tzu because they are floppy. It is common for yeast infections to form in your dog's ears, so check them whenever you check their eyes. Yeast infections can oc-

QUOTE
Health

According to the American Kennel Club (AKC), because of their heavy double coats and short faces, "Shih Tzu do not tolerate heat well and are not good swimmers." This breed is "generally healthy" but has a genetic predisposition to hip dysplasia, patellar luxation ("a slipped kneecap"), and several eye issues. Discuss these matters with your breeder before purchasing your dog. It is also a good idea to see the parents of the dog if possible.

Photo Courtesy of Lisa Agnew

cur throughout your dog's body, but their ears are the most common place for them to start. Similar to eye problems, don't just wait around if you see an issue. Contact your vet as soon as possible to stop the infection from getting worse.

Since Shih Tzu have flat faces, it is common for them to have breathing problems. Because of this, they can also get heatstroke fairly easily. If it is really hot outside, make sure not to walk your dog for long periods of time. Some symptoms of heatstroke are dizziness and even passing out. If this happens, take your dog to a cool area right away. You can apply cool towels to their body or set them near a fan to help cool them down faster as well. In general, whenever you take them on long walks, make sure to bring plenty of water for them in case they begin to pant heavily. While walks are healthy for your dog, you definitely do not want to overwork them. Instead of taking one long walk a day, consider taking them on multiple short walks if that seems like a better pace for them.

According to Shih Tzu breeder Stefanie Marie Peacock, of the genetic health problems Shih Tzu puppies face, "the most common is the Umbilical Hernia and Stenotic Nares." These conditions may sound scary, but are usually nothing to worry about because the vet will fix them when your dog gets spayed or neutered. The Umbilical Hernia is a bubble of fatty tissue that will appear on your dog's belly where your dog's umbilical cord was. The reason this happens so often with Shih Tzu is because they usually have an uneven bite and the moms will be stubborn and try to bite the umbilical cord off themselves. Breeders will try their best to assist with this part of the process, but sometimes they can't help it if the Shih Tzu gets to it first. This issue will usually fix itself, but if need be, the vet will correct it when you get your dog fixed.

The Stenotic Nares, on the other hand, are when the Shih Tzu's nostrils are pinched too tightly together, making it hard for the Shih Tzu to breathe. These will typically be common while your puppy is teething. Monica Cox from Maple Lane Pups describes that the puppy's nostrils "will open as the puppy grows and the inflammation from teething goes

CHAPTER 13   Basic Health Care

away, they may get tight again as adult teeth come in." It may not happen the same for every single puppy, but it is a common issue for Shih Tzu owners to be aware of. In order to avoid your Shih Tzu having breathing problems during this time, make sure your puppy is still actively eating and drinking often, because this will help to keep the nostrils open like normal. Even if you are concerned about your dog's tight nostrils, it is important to wait until they are done teething to consider getting surgery done. You will have to expect the occasional sniffing and snorting from your Shih Tzu puppy, but this is just to help fix their nostrils. Stenotic Nares are a condition that will usually fix themselves, so they really should not be a huge concern, but they are something that you should occasionally keep an eye on as your Shih Tzu puppy goes through this process.

While many breeders agree that the Umbilical Hernia and Stenotic Nares are the most common issues for Shih Tzu puppies, one breeder, Debbie Heuston from Debbie's Darlings, points out that "some genetic health problems can be problems with knees popping out of place, keeping them from doing a lot of jumping on or off furniture is a main cause. Providing steps is a great preventative for that." Shih Tzu are commonly known to try jumping up next to their owners no matter where they're sitting. While this can seem adorable at first, the more often they do this, the more it can harm your dog's joints, specifically their knees. Therefore, if a piece of furniture seems too high for your Shih Tzu to reach, you may want to give in to your Shih Tzu's laziness and pick them up. This way, your Shih Tzu will stay healthier longer and not have pain in their legs as they grow up. Like Heuston suggests, steps can be a good thing to put next to a high bed or couch to make it easier for your dog to access. You can also just use any short object to serve as a type of step for your dog, but try your best to make these jumps easier for your dog.

CHAPTER 14
Aging Dog Care

A s your dog ages, you may need to start acting differently toward them. They will likely slow down and not be as playful as they used to be, but they still need the same love and affection as before. Keep a close eye on your dog's health as they grow older to ensure that they can live the longest and happiest life possible.

Illness and Injury Prevention

HELPFUL TIP
Joining a Shih Tzu Club

To learn more about your Shih Tzu, you might consider joining one of the many worldwide Shih Tzu Clubs. In the United States, check the websites of the American Kennel Club (akc.org) and the American Shih Tzu Club (shihtzu. org). The United Kingdom has various organizations that include The Kennel Club (thekennelclub.org.uk), The Scottish Kennel Club (sottishkennelclub.org), and Northern Counties Shih Tzu Club among many others. European dog owners love the Shih Tzu breed as well. You will find clubs in Finland, Germany, Denmark, Sweden, France, and the Netherlands to name just a few. From Canada to Australia, the Philippines to Puget Sound, you'll find kennel clubs devoted to the little "lion dog," the Shih Tzu. These kennel clubs "exist to protect and promote the interests and well-being of dogs."

A good way to help prepare for and prevent future injuries is to visit the vet more often. When your dog is young, once a year is perfectly fine for a checkup, but once your dog becomes a senior, you may want to visit every six months just to be completely sure that everything is still good with your dog. Your vet can also give you tips on how to better maintain your older dog's health.

A Shih Tzu's life span typically ranges from about ten to sixteen years old. They would usually be considered a senior around when they turn eight or nine, but every dog will age at slightly different rates. If you are ever concerned about your Shih Tzu starting to slow down, contact your vet for advice on how to better care for your senior dog.

Even if your dog is still young, it is a good idea to plan ahead. If you keep up on your dog's health throughout their whole life and plan for when they start to age, then it

Photo Courtesy of
Marsha Parham

is less likely that they will develop any significant illnesses when they get older. This involves keeping them clean, keeping them a healthy weight, and making sure they're happy throughout their life. If you constantly keep this in mind while caring for your Shih Tzu, then your dog will have a better chance of living a long life.

Of course, similar to any person, a long life is never guaranteed for your dog, but it is important for you to do everything you can to help them out. If you don't have the time and money to keep your dog in a healthy condition, then that may be a sign that a dog is not for you, so keep that in mind before adopting your Shih Tzu. Their life is in your hands and you do not want to do anything to unintentionally harm them.

Basics of Senior Dog Care

As many people know, dogs age at a much faster rate than humans do. One human year is about the equivalent of seven years for a dog. This means that their life is much shorter than yours, but luckily, smaller dogs tend to live longer than larger ones, so your Shih Tzu will hopefully be able to live a long life with you.

You may need to become more patient with your dog as the years go on. They will still need regular exercise and walks, but make sure you walk at their pace in order to avoid working them too hard. Since Shih Tzu are lazy to begin with, don't expect your dog to act drastically different as they grow old, but they will still get even lazier as they get older. If they no longer want to play and run around as much, then that is something you need to accept. Don't try to overwork your elderly dog.

If your Shih Tzu has dark coloring, then you will be able to see white or gray hair during their senior years. However, if their fur is mostly white to begin with, then they may not appear any older. Their hair will likely not be as soft as it used to be, but the more you brush your dog's hair, the better it will be to maintain their hair as they grow up.

Sometimes your senior dog's appetite may change. They may not want to eat as often or they might suddenly be pickier with their foods. You may need to cut down their meals to adjust to their appetite. There are also types of food that are specifically made to help senior dogs, so that might be a good option if your dog is no longer interested in their normal dog food.

Grooming

Even if your senior dog seems a bit less tolerant when it comes to grooming, keeping your older dog clean is a must. Check their eyes, ears, and skin more frequently to be on the lookout for anything unusual on their body. If you don't check your dog often, they could develop some type of condition that you are unaware of. If you keep your dog clean, then it will be easier to spot any unusual behaviors or conditions right when they occur.

You will still want to get your senior dog groomed often, but understand that it may take longer for the groomer to finish your dog. This is because they want to be careful not to injure your dog. Older dogs may have a hard time standing for the entire groom or may get irritated by the dryer, so the groomer will try their best to take their time and give your dog as many breaks as necessary. This is why it is important to find a groomer you trust, so that you know they will be cautious and patient with your older dog.

Whenever you go to a new groomer, make sure you tell them your dog's age. It may not seem important to you, but grooming a puppy is much different from grooming a senior dog. Also tell your groomer

Photo Courtesy of
Lisa DeMarco

about any medical concerns your dog has before they start grooming. This way, they know which areas of your dog are most sensitive and they will be careful to groom around these areas. If you do not inform your groomer about any health issues with your dog, then they could accidentally harm your senior dog without meaning to.

Sometimes groomers will turn down your senior dog for haircuts simply because they want to make sure your dog is not put in any danger. Older dogs can be more fragile and sometimes harder to work with, so at some point, it may be best for you to start maintaining your Shih Tzu's grooming needs on your own. You know your dog better than anyone else, so you will be the most careful when it comes to bathing and cleaning different areas of your dog.

Common Illnesses for Senior Dogs

For senior dogs in general, there are a lot of different illnesses and conditions to expect. The more you care for your dog's health when they're younger, the better off they will be as they age. One common illness for senior dogs is gum disease, due to the fact that many owners neglect to clean their dog's teeth on a regular basis. The older your dog gets, the more buildup they will get on their teeth and gums and the more likely they will be to get this disease.

A lot of dogs also get arthritis and joint diseases as they grow older, just as people often do. This is because the cartilage that protects their joints wears down over time, causing painful friction when they try to move. This can make walking harder for your dog and cause them to slow down as they get older. If your dog is overweight, they are more likely to get joint problems sooner. All dogs can get it, but if your dog is not a healthy weight, then they will have a heavier load on their joints, making it harder for them to move. If you notice your Shih Tzu having a hard time moving around, check in with your vet so that they can help to find a way to ease these pains for your dog.

If your dog is obese, then there are lots of other diseases that can come from that with old age. In addition to joint disease, they can also get diabetes and respiratory illnesses. It is more common for senior dogs to become overweight because they do not get as much exercise as a younger Shih Tzu would. To keep your senior dog from getting overweight, it may help to keep your dog on a strict diet once they reach an older age. This can help them to maintain a healthy weight even if they are not getting as much exercise as they should.

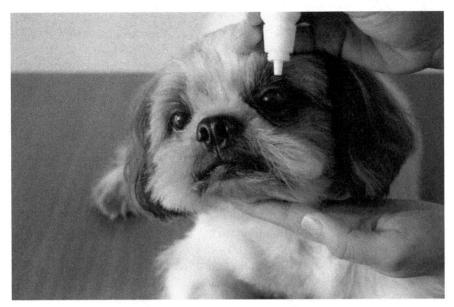

Another disease that older dogs can get is cancer, just like humans can. It is a common cause of death in older dogs, so it is an important condition to look out for. It can most commonly be spotted if there is a large lump on your dog that doesn't seem to heal. If there is any type of bump or swelling on your dog's skin that seems abnormal, then you may want to check with the vet to make sure it is not something serious. It would be better for you to know about the cancer ahead of time instead of losing your dog to this condition one day out of the blue. You also don't want your dog to suffer either.

When It's Time to Say Goodbye

It's hard to process the fact that your dog will not live forever. Over time, they will start to slow down and if your dog starts to act in a way that is greatly unlike them, then you may want to see the vet to make sure that everything is okay. It is normal for your dog to be lazier than usual, but if they become so lazy that they don't even want to get up at all, this could possibly mean that something is wrong with them. The sooner you can catch any symptoms in your dog, the easier it can be to find a cure.

There will be some signs that your dog's life is coming to an end simply based on their behavior. They can sometimes be in so much pain they can't even walk, so they might just want to lie around all the time. If

they can't even stand up long enough to go outside and go to the bathroom or they are refusing to either eat or drink, these are unfortunately signs that you need to accept that your dog does not need to live much longer. Try to allow your dog to have some fun experiences during their final few days so that they can at least make some last happy memories with you.

If your dog gets a disease that seems very severe, always consult your vet before deciding to let your dog go. Your dog could have a curable condition that you are unaware of, so it is always good to find out all the facts in case there is a way to allow your dog to live longer. However, if you can tell that your dog is in a lot of pain, then sometimes it is better to put them out of their misery. As hard as it can be to let your dog go, you just need to remember that you gave your dog a long and happy life and that's what matters.

It can be hard to watch your dog go, but when it comes time to, the best thing to do is to be right by your dog's side through the whole process. You don't want your dog's last moments to be spent looking around for you and not knowing where you are. If you are at their side, they will be more relaxed and happy because you are nearby. It is a very hard experience to go through, but every dog owner must do it at some point. Don't let the sad moments such as this one distract you from the excitement you will feel throughout your Shih Tzu's life.

Overall, the Shih Tzu is an excellent breed to keep as a pet. If you are looking for a small, hypoallergenic dog that will give you lots of love, then a Shih Tzu may just be the perfect pet for you. They are friendly, loyal, and always willing to keep you company and care for you when needed. They love to protect their owners and make sure those they care about are safe at all times. They have the energy to keep life exciting for you as well as the laziness to give you plenty of cuddles. They can be a handful from time to time, but if you decide to bring a Shih Tzu into your life, it will be a decision that you will never regret.

CPSIA information can be obtained
at www.ICGtesting.com
Printed in the USA
BVHW051815250122
627121BV00003B/133